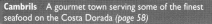

Cambrils A gourmet town serving some of the finest seafood on the Costa Dorada *(page 58)*

Sant Pol The beach scene at this village has a low-key charm *(page 25)*

Ebro Delta A large wetland with excellent birdwatching opportunities *(page 60)*

Pont del Diable A striking Roman aqueduct just north of Tarragona *(page 45)*

Altafulla The picturesque, narrow streets are a pleasure to explore *(page 43)*

Salou A family-orientated resort town with a good range of facilities *(page 56)*

CONTENTS

57

12

87

10

72

20

INTRODUCTION

The Costa Dorada takes its name from those fine, golden *(dorada)* beaches that stretch almost continuously for over 240km (150 miles) along this calm Mediterranean shoreline. Technically the Costa Dorada begins in the south at the Ebro Delta and ends some 16km (10 miles) north of Sitges, where the Costa del Garraf begins. This continues north as the Costa de Barcelona, before becoming the Costa del Maresme. This guide covers the region from just south of the Ebro Delta up to and including the Maresme.

The Costa Dorada forms the southern shore of Catalonia, a large, autonomous (though not independent) part of Spain which stretches north to the French border and far west across the Pyrenees.

Catalan name

Costa Dorada is known in Spain by its local Catalan name, *Costa Daurada*. Visitors should also note that the Catalan for Catalonia is *Catalunya*.

A Place Apart

Catalonia is different to the rest of Spain, not least in its language, Catalan, a Romance language which is used officially and spoken almost everywhere. Whereas southern Spain was influenced by the Moors, the north of the country has always looked towards Europe. Andalusians may dance the fiery *flamenco*, but Catalans hold hands in a circle for the stately *sardana*. Spanish traditions mean less here; the *siesta* is largely eschewed in favour of work, or an active lunch-break. Notably also, bullfighting is not a Catalan pastime. Catalans like to go their own way, and they defend their right to do so with

Cambrils, fishing port-turned-resort

Café life

a passion; just talk to them about Catalan history, or food, attend any *fiesta*, or watch a Barcelona football match in a crowded bar, and you'll soon see (or hear) the independent spirit for which the whole area is renowned.

Towns and Resorts

The major metropolis of Catalonia is Barcelona. This lively, fashionable city boasts a fascinating Gothic Quarter, over 40 museums, art from antiquity to Gaudí and Miró, and restaurants and nightlife to rival the best in Europe. What's more, it is also a booming economic centre; Barcelona produces almost 20 percent of Spain's industrial output.

There is, however, another main city on the Costa Dorada relatively unknown to international tourism. During Roman times, Tarragona was the most influential city on the whole of the Iberian Peninsula. Now its Roman legacy includes some of the finest monuments surviving from this period. Walk around the city walls, stroll under the great aqueduct, look down upon the once-bloody amphitheatre, and admire the museums and mosaics – Roman history comes alive in old 'Tarraco'. There's also a fascinating medieval quarter here, and at its heart, one of Spain's finest cathedrals. Tarragona offers more than history, though, from its lively Rambla to excellent beaches and good restaurants. Best of all, if you want to avoid other holidaymakers, it is relatively undiscovered.

One consequence of Tarragona's relative anonymity is the shortage of good medium-priced accommodation. Salou provides a good solution, however, and offers masses of affordable accommodation a mere 10- to 15-minute bus ride away. Better still might be Cambrils, the salubrious neighbour of Salou, a charming fishing port-turned-resort which is justly famous all over Catalonia for its fish restaurants.

Further north, don't miss a visit to Sitges. It's the most complete resort on the Costa Dorada and is famous for letting its hair down, particularly at Carnival time – but then any *fiesta* around here is worth attending.

Some of the old fishing villages along the coast have become real tourist 'meccas'. But you can still find small towns where the main source of income is the sea, whose growth is controlled and where the objective is to preserve the best of the bygone days of these typical fishing ports.

You'll find the food is good all along the coast. Fish and seafood are nearly always the speciality on the menu, from

On the sands at Sitges

Medieval Montblanc

exotic *paellas* and seafood stews to simple grilled fish, served with Tarragona's uniquely delicious *romesco* sauce *(see page 100)*.

The Costa Dorada is also renowned for its wines. Just north of Tarragona lies one of Spain's finest wine-producing areas, the Penedès. Here too are the *bodegas* that produce Spain's famous sparkling *cava*. A trip to the market town of Vilafranca del Penedés and then to a *cava* producer makes for an excellent day out.

Secluded Settings

Further inland, northwest of Barcelona, is the 10th-century Benedictine monastery of Montserrat – a must, not just for its religious trappings, but also for its seclusion and magical mountain setting.

The 12th-century Cistercian monasteries of Santes Creus and Poblet, meanwhile, conjure up the authentic atmosphere of an altogether different period, when the kingdom of Catalonia was the most powerful in the Mediterranean. These monasteries lie nestled between the coastal plain and the wild Prades Mountains, a haven for walkers and climbers. Nearby are the picturesque towns of Reus and Montblanc, both well worth exploring, while peace and quiet can also be enjoyed by heading south to the Ebro Delta, a wild and wonderful wetland where flamingos roost and rice is grown.

A BRIEF HISTORY

The first people to inhabit Catalonia were Palaeolithic hunters who left their mark through cave paintings at Ulldecona, south of the Ebro Delta. Neolithic and Bronze Age relics have also turned up in the region around Tarragona, where cattle-rearing and agriculture were practised.

The Greeks and Phoenicians brought commerce and culture to Catalonia, while the Carthaginians are said to have given Barcelona its original name, Barcino, in honour of the general Hamilcar Barca, father of Hannibal. Barca established his base in 237BC and moved south, establishing a further stronghold at Tarragona and subjugating much of the country south of the Ebro Delta. His son, Hannibal, was to lose it all some 20 years later, however, when he provoked the Romans into entering Catalonia to embark upon the Second Punic War.

The Spanish Roman Empire

It was Cneus Cornelius Scipio who first established a military presidium at Tarraco (Roman for Tarragona) and used it as a base from where he could attack Hannibal's forces. After 16 years of battle, Scipio's army was victorious and Hannibal fled into exile (later to commit suicide).

Tarraco was established as the capital of the new region, and continued to be a military centre of command, directing operations to annex all Hispanic territories to the Roman Empire. It was

Roman aqueduct in Tarragona

considered an ideal point for a number of reasons: not only was it the main port on the sea routes between the Italian peninsula and the Hispanic northeast, but it also held an advanced position for penetrating both east and south. Last, but not least, it enjoyed a very pleasant climate.

It took almost 200 years to subdue the native tribes in the central and northern areas of present-day Spain, but eventually the Roman country was to prosper. Tarragona enjoyed particular prominence during the reign of Julius Caesar, who called the settlement Colonia Julia Victrix Triumphalis to commemorate his victories. The Romans initially divided the peninsula into two: Hispaniae Ulterior and Hispaniae Citerior ('Further' and 'Nearer' respectively). In 27BC, during the reign of Emperor Augustus, the Iberian Peninsula was reorganised to form three provinces: Tarraconensis (covering north, northwest and central Spain); Lusitania (approximating to modern

Sundial at the amphitheatre in Tarragona

Portugal); and Baetica (southern Spain). Tarraconensis was the largest province, and as its capital Tarraco coined its own money and boasted two forums (one for the local council, one for the provincial) and a number of monuments, many of which still remain. The vaults for the circus tiers, the magnificent aqueduct, the Roman am-

Tarraco's triumph

The emperors Hadrian and Trajan, both born in Spain, endowed Tarraco with power and cultural prestige, while its flax trade and other industries made it one of the Roman Empire's richest seaports. The region's wines were commended by none other than Pliny the Elder.

phitheatre, and the sturdy Prætori building all attest to the importance of Tarraco at the height of the Spanish Roman Empire. Of course, the Romans also left their language, with Latin forming the basis of Catalan.

Tarragona was also to be an important centre in the spread of Christianity across the region. There is a strong belief that St Paul preached in the city, and in AD259, the bishop of Tarraco became the earliest Christian martyr on the peninsula when he was burned alive in the amphitheatre. Some four centuries later, this gruesome event was commemorated by the erection of a Visigothic basilica on the site, the ruins of which still remain.

Visigoths and Moors

By the 5th century, Rome's grip had slackened and Spain was besieged by the Vandals and the Visigoths. Although Barcelona and Tarragona were sacked, the Visigoths, who had been allies of Rome, did establish a sort of civilised order, which lasted until AD711. In the same year, a Moorish army was foolishly invited into the country and, not content with the role of mere mercenaries, the Muslim forces assailed the entire Iberian Peninsula, and Catalonia was briefly overrun.

Wilfred the Hairy gave the budding Catalan nation its flag of four horizontal red stripes on a gold field, the oldest still in use in Europe. Legend holds that the stripes were etched in Wilfred's blood, drawn on his shield by the fingers of the Frankish king after the count had defended his overlord in a battle.

However, the Moors were defeated beyond the Pyrenees by Charlemagne's Franks in AD732, and withdrew to the south.

In AD878, under the patronage of the Franks, Guifré el Pélos (Wilfred the Hairy) became Count of Barcelona, so founding a dynasty that would rule for nearly five centuries. The Barcelona counts declared their independence from the Moors in 988; Tarragona, meanwhile, sacked then abandoned by the Moors, was not reclaimed by Christian forces until Count Ramón Berenguer III set about expanding the Catalan empire in the early 11th century.

Catalonia's Golden Age

In the early Middle Ages, Catalonia prospered. It received its own constitution and, with expedient marriages, managed to form unions with Provence and Aragón. Expansion overseas took off in 1229 when Jaume I set sail from Salou to dislodge the Moors from the Balearics. His son, Pedro III, was later to add Sicily to the growing empire.

By the 14th century, lands controlled by Catalonia included much of what is today southern France, as well as Sardinia and Corsica, and for a time the kingdom of Catalonia was the most powerful in the Mediterranean. This too was an era of bold architecture, as evidenced by the cathedrals of Tarragona and Barcelona, and the Cistercian abbeys of Poblet and Santes Creus. The arts flourished, patronised by a vigorous class of bankers and merchants, including important Jewish communities. Nascent political institutions

The cloister at Santes Creus

appeared, and in 1359 the Corts Catalanes, or Catalan Parliament, which had been meeting irregularly since the 1280s, was officially appointed.

Hard Times

The marriage of Ferdinand of Aragón-Catalonia (Ferrán II to the Catalans) to Isabella of Castile in 1469 joined the two crowns and formed the nucleus of a united Spanish state. Under the Catholic Monarchs Catalonia was incorporated into Castile. The Catholic church's hard-line Inquisition expelled Jews from Spain, and the Jewish population of Barcelona completely disappeared, while Tarragona's was hugely reduced. The discovery of the Americas by Columbus in 1492 was also to prove disastrous for Catalonia. The Mediterranean lost some of its importance as a trading zone, while the southern ports swiped the rich transatlantic business. The 16th century was a Golden Age for Spain, but the political influence of Catalonia and Barcelona was on the wane, and after Madrid became the capital of Spain in 1556, it declined even further.

During the 17th century, Catalonia was a troubled land, rebelling against King Philip IV and siding with Spain's enemy, France. In 1652, after 12 years of fighting, Barcelona gave in and renewed its allegiance to Spain. But 50 years later Catalonia again took the wrong side, this time in the War of the Spanish Succession, and was punished. Both the Catalan Parliament and the language were banned.

In the second half of the 18th century, Charles III rescued the region from a trading slump by opening up profitable trade routes with Latin America. Tarragona prospered as a major wine blending and export centre, the profits from which were ploughed back in to a now burgeoning Catalan textile trade.

War and Peace

For Catalonia and Spain, the 19th century seemed to be one long series of wars, starting with the War of Independence in 1808 and ending in 1898 with the Spanish-American War.

Modernisme

Despite the uncertain political times of the late 19th century, the arts were flourishing, with the movement known as Modernisme (the Spanish form of Art Nouveau) at the fore.

A rebellion against the rigid form and colourless stone and plaster of the classical architecture that had replaced Gothic, the style thrived (and has subsequently been preserved) in Catalonia, and particularly in Barcelona. Gaudí's Barcelona works are legendary, but elsewhere in the region you will also see many fine examples of this school, from grand lines and designs on the most elegant public buildings to simple adornments gracing humbler homes.

Yet despite that, Catalan industry developed ahead of the rest of Spain. The country's first railway was built in 1848 along the Costa del Maresme, from Barcelona to Mataró, and then extended to Tarragona. Towards the end of the century, the cava industry began bubbling in earnest, and Barcelona expanded rapidly.

The century finished with general disillusionment as to the ability and role of the royalty, but, with no democratic structure to replace it, the 20th century ushered in increasing working-class political dissatisfaction and a failing economy. Confusion, disorder and even anarchy

Modernist creation: Palau de la Música in Barcelona

were growing. King Alfonso XIII was succeeded by General Primo de Rivera in 1923 in a military coup, but he brought no respite to the country's ailing condition, and after seven years the general fell. Elections in 1931 brought the Republican Party to power and Catalonia briefly won back its autonomy.

The Franco Years

The following five years were scarred by violent demonstrations and strikes until 1936, when General Francisco Franco led a military insurrection that soon became a bitter and bloody civil war. Catalonia remained fiercely Republican while Barcelona was bombed by Italian fighters.

The bloodiest battle of all was at the Ebro near Tortosa *(see page 64)*. Barcelona fell in 1939, and Catalonia was reabsorbed into Spain. Within two months the war had ended, having claimed 750,000 lives. Once again Catalonia's autonomy was lost and its language was banned.

After keeping Spain out of World War II, Franco was assisted in the rebuilding of the economy post-war by the advent of mass tourism and the 1953 American Aid plan (in exchange for land for air-force bases). He died in 1975, but not without ensuring that his successor would be Juan Carlos, grandson of Alfonso XIII.

Modern Times

A period of transition followed, during which Spain, with the full cooperation of Juan Carlos, became a democracy. In 1976 the first elections for 40 years were held. Catalonia was also given back its autonomy.

As if to remind the world that Spain was still a fledgling democracy, a coup in 1981 failed largely thanks to the intervention of the king. In 1986 Spain joined the EC (now the EU), and since then has benefited enormously from investment, including the development of tourism along the 'costas'. Today, Barcelona has become one of the fastest-growing of Western Europe's economies, a status enhanced by the success of the 1992 Olympic Games. Meanwhile, into the 21st century, Catalonia remains without doubt one of Spain's most exciting regions to visit.

The Catalan flag

Historical Landmarks

237BC Carthaginian general Hamilcar Barca makes his base at Barcino (Barcelona).

206BC Romans establish a military base at Tarraco (Tarragona).

27BC Tarraco made capital of the Roman province of Hispania Citerior.

AD259 Bishop of Tarraco is burned alive in amphitheatre.

531–54 Barcelona becomes capital of the Visigoths.

711 Moorish invasion of Spain.

878 Guifré el Pélos (Wilfred the Hairy) becomes Count of Barcelona.

1096–1131 Ramón Berenguer III extends the Catalan empire.

1229 Jaume I consolidates the empire and expands Barcelona.

1359 Corts Catalanes (Parliament of Catalonia) established.

1469 Ferdinand and Isabella unite Aragón and Castile.

1494 Administration of Catalonia put under Castilian control.

1516 Carlos I (Charles V, Holy Roman Emperor) takes the throne.

1639 Catalonia sides with France in the Thirty Year' War.

1659 Catalan territories north of Pyrenees ceded to France.

1701–13 War of Spanish Succession.

1914 Mancomunitat (provincial government) formed in Catalonia.

1923 General Primo de Rivera sets up military dictatorship, bans the Catalan language and dissolves the Mancomunitat.

1931 Republican Party comes to power.

1932 Catalonia granted autonomy.

1938 Battle of the Ebro.

1939 Civil War ends in victory for General Franco; Catalonia loses its autonomy.

1975 Franco dies; Juan Carlos becomes king.

1978 Statute of Autonomy; Catalan restored as official language.

1986 Spain joins the European Community (now European Union).

1992 The Olympics are held in Barcelona.

2000 The Archaeological Ensemble of Tarraco declared a Unesco World Heritage Site.

2008 Barcelona connected with Madrid by high-speed AVE rail service.

WHERE TO GO

Spain's glittering northern Mediterranean coastline casts an alluring spell. This guide takes the Costa del Meresme as its starting point, and heads south through the city of Barcelona to find its main focus in the resorts, towns and villages of the Costa Dorada, before ending just past the Ebro Delta in the Costa del Azahar. Many visitors wishing to explore this region rent a car. Trains offer an excellent alternative – a good rail service runs right along the coast.

THE COSTA DEL MARESME

The area of the Costa del Maresme stretches some 38km (24 miles) from Mataró, north of Barcelona, to the Río Tordero, where the Costa Brava begins. Maresme means a low-lying coastal region susceptible to flooding, and it could hardly be in more complete contrast to the rugged cliffs of the neighbouring coast.

The beaches here are long and narrow, and often divided from the towns whose name they bear by the railway and busy N11 road that run parallel to the coast. (To reach the beach you first have to find the subway) In many places, the Costa del Maresme is less developed than the Costa Dorada, and is almost exclusively the retreat of Spanish holidaymakers. The train is also a boon to anyone who wants to avoid the famous traffic jams. At weekends and during the summer holidays, the N11 is bumper-to-bumper with frustrated Barcelonans.

The first resort of note, **Vilassar de Mar**, has a spacious beach, but it is the small town itself that is really of interest.

Platja Varador, Mataró

Look for the well-preserved, 16th-century **watchtower** on the main road. This is just one of many along this coast and is a legacy of the days when the inhabitants lived in fear of raiding corsairs. Close by is a group of fine **19th-century houses** which carry flamboyant hallmarks of *Modernisme (see page 16)*; these are good examples of the type of building typical to this area.

Mataró

With a population of 120,000, **Mataró** is by far the biggest town on the Maresme. It's not a resort, but it does have a good beach, and you might wish to explore the old part of this once-walled town. The **basílica of Santa María** is the most notable of several baroque buildings here. In addition, you can't help but notice the fruit and vegetable crops by the roadside – thanks to the fertile soil, the Maresme region is

Basílica of Santa María in Mataró

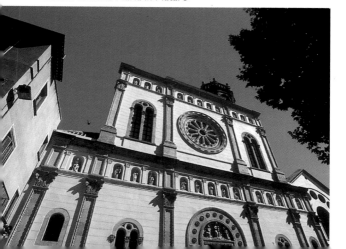

known as 'the vegetable garden of Barcelona'.

If you enjoy watching
sleek new yachts and power-
boats, drop in at Mataró's
impressive marina, where
there is berthing for over
1,000 vessels. In fact, this
small stretch of the Maresme
is highly popular with the
yachting fraternity; El Masnou, Premiá de Mar, El Balis
and Arenys De Mar also
have sizeable marinas.

Arenys port

Caldes d'Estrac

Although there's a pleasant beach at Sant Andreu de Lla-
vaneres, it's worth continuing a little further to the more up-
market **Caldes d'Estrac** (also known as Caldetes) for a
leisurely stop. Lavish turn-of-the-20th-century Catalan seaside villas and smart restaurants line the palm-fringed *passeig maritim* (promenade) backed by green hills. The beach
has been divided into sections by stone breakwaters that
form small crescents of sand. The Romans were the first to
bathe here, though not in the sea, but in the same 39°C
(102°F) mineral waters which also led the Edwardians to establish a resort here.

Arenys de Mar

Arenys de Mar has been a seafaring town since the 16th century, and although the new marina is now an international
focus of attention for regattas, the old port is still full of character and offers a good supply of fish restaurants. There is a
beautiful beach where you can sleep off your fish lunch, and

the town itself, dominated by its long, wide, tree-lined Rambla, is well worth a visit. On the Rambla is a fine parish church renowned for its elaborate (some say over-elaborate) baroque altarpiece. Wander as well through the narrow, old streets and be sure to visit the small **Museu Mares de la Punta**, which is reputed to be one of the best museums dedicated to fine lace in Europe. Another local speciality is *Calisay*, a brand of orange liqueur which is made in the centre of town. Inquire at the tourist office for details on guided tours of distilleries.

Canet de Mar

Canet de Mar is a straightforward seaside resort on the N11 road. It calls itself the *Vila Catalana del Modernisme* (the Catalan town of Modernism, *see page 16*) and claims some 60 Modernist buildings. The centrepiece is the **Casa Museu**

Casa Museu of Lluís Domènech i Montaner

(Tue–Fri 9am–2pm, Sat–Sun 10am–2pm; charge) in the former home of Lluís Domènech i Montaner, who lived all his life in Canet de Mar. Well known as a follower of the school of *Modernisme*, he designed a number of fine buildings in Barcelona, including the Casa Lleó Morera and the stunning Palau de la Música Catalana.

Sant Pol

Sant Pol

Sant Pol de Mar is probably the most charming village along the Costa del Maresme. Narrow, winding streets lead up to the 16th-century **Esglesia de Sant Jaume** and a 15th-century watchtower perched high above the beach. Down below, you can change for the beach in Victorian bathing huts, rent an old-fashioned deckchair with arm supports, and sink into a beach scene which, apart from the style of the bathing costumes, has changed little in a century.

Callella

The king of the coast is without doubt **Callella** (also called Callella de la Costa so as to distinguish it from Callella de Palafrugell on the Costa Brava). Driving to it from the south, the approach is distinguished by a **lighthouse**, quite remote from the seashore, high on a rocky cliff above the road. Opposite is a lay-by where curious spectators peer down some 18–24m (60–80ft) at the prettiest and smallest of Callella's beaches. (The beach is also popular with naturists, which may of course be the reason for the crowds above.)

Callella lighthouse

As the cliff-hugging road swings to the left, the vast expanse of Callella's **main beach** is revealed on the opposite side of the road in all its panoramic glory. The vast, wide, golden sands are neatly punctuated by high-tech beach-bar awnings, and during the summer you'll find they are chock-a-block with truly dedicated sunbathers.

The resort generally bustles with tourist development and there is now little left of the old settlement. The **Municipal Arxiu** (archive), housed in a fine old building, is worth a look, as is the pretty church. On your way to the beach, by the railway lines, there is still some fine typical Catalan seaside-resort architecture.

Callella sprawls south along the coast and finally collides with **Pineda de Mar** and **Santa Susanna**. Pineda has a particularly good beach. The final town of any size on the Costa del Maresme is **Malgrat de Mar**. With its 3km (2 miles) of beach, it is popular with Spanish and foreign tourists alike, but as an industrial town it holds less general appeal than some of its neighbours. However, there are two notable attractions nearby: **Marineland** *(see page 92)* and **Castell Medieval** at the town of **Tordera**. The latter belongs to the Comte de Valltordera, and you can go back to the days of chivalry here, enjoying a tournament while tucking into a medieval banquet (www.castellmedieval.com). There's also the church of Sant Esteve to admire, which dates from the 10th century.

BARCELONA

Barcelona is a sophisticated city where the creative energy of modern Europe and the relaxed pleasures of the Mediterranean meet in happy union. It may be Spain's second city, but it is very definitely a capital, though now of a culture rather than a country. Barcelona's avenues, broad and leafy, boast plazas, statues and fountains at the main intersections. Few skyscrapers intrude on the human scale of the city profile. The buildings which leave an impression are usually banks; almost as numerous as the bars, they are a reminder that for all its southern European flair, this is also a city of big business.

Go straight to the famous **Rambla** – half promenade and half bazaar – to catch the feeling of the city. There's a bustle and energy here which is unmatched almost anywhere else in Europe. The Rambla is also a good point of orientation. At

Barcelona La Rambla

Bus Turistic

For an easy introduction to the city, jump aboard the Bus Turistic. This is an excellent hop-on hop-off service which takes in the most interesting parts. The fare also entitles you to free cable-car, funicular, and tram rides, and to discounts on admission to several attractions – pick up a leaflet from any tourist office. The ride starts at Plaça de Catalunya, and tickets can be purchased on the bus. You can take either a north or south route.

the bottom is the seaport, to the east is the cathedral and the Barri Gòtic (the Gothic/ Medieval Quarter), at the top end is the 19th-century city, famous for its Modernist architecture, and to the west rises **Montjuïc**, hub of the dazzling 1992 Olympics.

The Rambla

The beginning of the Rambla is marked by the statue of Christopher Columbus, on top of his 50m (164ft) **Monument a Colom**. If you are interested in seafaring history, do not miss the **Museu Marítim** (near the monument), which chronicles over seven centuries of shipbuilding in Barcelona. Take a look out over the waterfront: there is a cable car here – the **Transbordador Aeri** – swinging above the harbour to the dockside area, **La Barceloneta**, famous for its fish restaurants and endowed with a landscaped promenade behind its newly created beaches.

La Rambla stretches nearly 1.5km (1 mile) up a gentle incline to the very hub of the city, the **Plaça de Catalunya**. It changes its name seamlessly five times from top to bottom.

Near the bottom of the Rambla is the **Barrí Xino** (Chinatown), once notoriously seedy and dangerous and still best avoided by night. A little further along and just off the Rambla is the **Palau Güell**, a splendid mansion built by Gaudí in 1885 for his principal patron, the textile tycoon Count Eusebi Güell. On the opposite side of the Rambla is **Plaça**

Reial. Although it has a number of good bars and restaurants, this arcaded square is still the haunt of down-and-outs, but is now attempting to regain its fashionable image of former years. Also on this stretch of the Rambla you'll start to encounter street entertainers: musicians, fire-eaters, human statues, jugglers and a host of other eccentric performers.

The next building of note is the **Gran Teatre del Liceu** – a monument of the Catalan *Renaixença* period. Opened in 1847, the Liceu was one of Europe's most beautiful opera houses, until it was gutted by fire in 1994. Restoration and extension work was completed in 1999. Across the street is the venerable **Café del'Opera**, established in 1876. With its elegant décor, this is a nice place to stop for some refreshment.

Rambla de les Flors

The heart of the Rambla is the **Pla de la Boqueria** – its 19th-century covered market, known as **La Boqueria** (Mon–Sat 8am–8.30pm), is a city highlight. Huge mounds of fruit, vegetables, sausages, meat, poultry, seafood, herbs, spices and sweetmeats form a cornucopian mosaic under the building's high-ceilinged, ironwork naves.

The next part of the Rambla is famous for its flowers and is one of the most photographed scenes in the city. The blossoms give way to birds and their vendors and the Rambla finishes at **Plaça de Catalunya**.

Barrí Gòtic and the Born

If you step off the Rambla about half-way along and walk east, you will find yourself in the **Barrí Gòtic** – the oldest part of town. This is an atmospheric area of narrow alleyways and old buildings, many of which have been regenerated as museums, hotels or restaurants. You'll find the best bits in a well-preserved concentration of medieval architecture clustered around the **Catedral de Santa Eulalia**. It was begun in the 13th century, though its Gothic facade was not finished until 1892. Don't miss the beautiful cloister.

Next door is the **Palau Reial** (Royal Palace), famed as the place where Columbus met Ferdinand and Isabella in 1493 to report what he had found in the New World.

Catedral de Santa Eulalia

There are also two excellent museums here. The **Museu d'Història de la Ciutat** (Museum of the History of the City; Tue–Sat 10am–8pm in summer and 10am–2pm and 4–7pm in winter, Sun 10am–3pm; charge) is located in a rebuilt 15th-century mansion. In the basement you can walk over the extensive ruins of Roman Barcelona. The **Museu Frederic Marés** is a wonderfully eclectic collection of religious objects, art and miscellany.

Just outside the Barri Gòtic is the Born, a district which contains Barcelona's most popular museum, the

Museu Picasso (Tue–Sun 10am–8pm; charge; www.museu picasso.bcn.es). Devoted to the works of the great artist, it occupies several splendid palaces in the Carrer de Montcada, one of the medieval city's best-preserved streets. Unfortunately, you won't see Picasso's greatest works in here, and there are few Cubist pieces, but it is nonetheless an excellent collection.

Continue south along the Carrer de Montcada to reach one of the city's finest churches, **Santa María del Mar**. As the name suggests, at this point you are almost back on the waterfront. It is a short walk to the harbour with its shopping centre, aquarium and IMAX cinema. Just to the east of here is the **Ciutadella**, named after a prison erected by the French in 1714, and torn down with much glee in 1869. It is now a lovely, mature park, famous as the site of **Barcelona Zoo**, and home to performing dolphins and a killer whale.

L'Eixample

The Rambla ends at **Plaça de Catalunya**. To the north of this central square is the district known as **L'Eixample** ('the expansion', built largely between 1860 and 1920). This area is famous for its Modernist architecture, and the buildings not to miss are all on Passeig de Gràcia, which runs north from one corner of the plaça. Note in particular: No. 35, **Casa Lleó Morera**, by Domènech i Montaner; No. 41, **Casa Amatller** by Puig i Cadafalch; No. 43, **Casa Batlló** by Gaudí; and No. 92, **Casa Milà** (also known as La Pedrera) by Gaudí. The latter two are both extraordinary buildings, with all of Gaudí's inventive, surrealist hallmarks. The buildings' interiors can be visited.

For more of the master of *Modernisme*, rejoin the bus to the city's most famous landmark, the church of the **Sagrada Família** (Holy Family). No matter how many pictures you have seen of this masterpiece-in-progress, you won't be disappointed by the reality.

The basic shape is firmly rooted in Barcelona's Gothic tradition, but no other Gothic church has stonework that drips like melted candlewax, or sculptures of snails, vines and tortoises, or 100m (330ft) towers that resemble perforated cigars. A lift and steps take you all the way up to view the detail on the towers, including Gaudí's famous 'broken-plate mosaics'.

The church is unfinished, and as Gaudí's plans were destroyed during the Civil War, no-one knows what his exact intentions were. Work continues, but at a snail's pace. Sagrada Família is due for completion in 2026, the centenary of Gaudí's death.

More of Gaudí's work can be found north of Sagrada Família at the **Parc Güell**. His patron, Count Güell, intended to create a community of villas here within the 2.5-hectare (6-acre) park, and in 1900 gave Gaudí carte blanche to produce an original design. The result is a compendium

Gaudí's Casa Batlló on Passeig de Gràcia

of the designer's most distinctive devices – dragons, stout columns (86 of them supporting the roof of what was to have been the colony's covered market), a serpentine wall and tiled mosaic bench around a raised plaza, and mask-eyes as windows. However, the villa plan never took off, and the property became a family park in 1923. Here is also the house in which Gaudí lived for a while, which now serves as a museum.

View from the spire of Sagrada Família

Montjuïc

In 1992 **Montjuïc** ('Hill of the Jews'), to the west of the city centre, was transformed into a new Mount Olympus as millions of television viewers thrilled to pictures of highboard divers perched spectacularly above the city at the open-air Olympic swimming pool. The hill is no stranger to big events. In 1929 it was the site of the International Exhibition, at which time the ornate fountains of the **Plaça d'Espanya** were created to grace the entrance. The gateway is also marked by two, huge brick columns modelled on St Mark's campanile in Venice. Several large hangar-type halls, still used for commercial exhibitions, lead up to the **Palau Nacional**. This was the Spanish Pavilion in 1929 and now houses the **Museu d'Art de Catalunya** (Tue–Sat 10am–7pm, Sun 10am–2.30pm; charge) containing one of the world's finest collections of Romanesque and Gothic art.

Palau Nacional

There are so many attractions on Montjuïc alone that it would be easy to spend several days here. Chief among them is the **Poble Espanyol** (Spanish Village) where you can see the whole of Spain in a couple of hours. The village is a showcase of the country's various regions, each of which are represented by miniature replicas of houses, churches, fountains, plazas and palaces. There are 115 of them in total, interspersed with shops, restaurants, tapas bars and artisans' workshops.

If you are in search of more cerebral diversions, there are plenty of other museums and galleries on Montjuïc. In particular, don't miss the witty, abstract art of the highly rated **Fundació Miró** (Tue–Sat 10am–7pm, until 8pm in summer, Thur 10am–9.30pm, Sun 10am–2.30pm; charge).

Take the bus to the cable car, the **Telefèric de Montjuïc**, which takes you on a breathtaking ride high above the Olympic swimming pool and the city skyline to the summit of the hill, where there is the impressive 17th-century **Castell**

de Montjuïc, which houses a military museum.

If you get a bright, clear day and want a view of Barcelona that puts Montjuïc into a different perspective, catch the bus to **Tibidabo** and change onto the city's last tram service. The famous 1900-vintage **tramvia blau** (blue tram) takes you almost to the top of this 542m (1,778ft) peak overlooking Barcelona, then it's another 5-minute trip on the funicular to the summit. There's a good amusement park here combining the best of old- and new-technology rides.

Further Sights

If you still have a desire to see religious buildings, visit the **Monestir de Pedralbes** (Tue–Sun 10am– 2pm), named after its white stones. It is situated on the

German Pavilion

Near to the Palau Nacional is the Pavelló Mies van der Rohe, the Modernist German Pavilion built by Ludwig Mies van der Rohe for the 1929 Barcelona World Fair. It was for this event that the architect designed his now-iconic 'Barcelona' chair, created as a throne for the Spanish royals.

northeastern edge of the city centre and has a superb Gothic church and a charming three-storey cloister.

A temple to an altogether different Spanish passion, although one that is hardly less devout, lies just south of here. The 120,000-seat **Camp Nou Stadium** is famous all over the football-loving world as the home of Barcelona FC. There are tours of both the ground and of the Museu del Futbol.

The beach at Sitges

BARCELONA TO TARRAGONA

The first resort along the coast south of Barcelona is **Castell-defells**, whose long, wide, sandy beach has made it popular.

Sitges

Beyond Castelldefells, take either the section of motorway called *Tunels de Garraf*, which cuts through the mountain, or follow the coast road, which winds its way along the cliffs, skirting a number of industrial installations before reaching the tiny resort of **Garraf**. This is a neat and tidy place, where old-fashioned green and white beach houses look out to sea, and smart villas blend into a mountainous backdrop. Continue along the coast road, and within a couple of kilometres of each other are two new marinas *(ports esportius)*. The first, close to Garraf, is **Port Ginesta**, and the second, **Port Aiguadolç**, is a lively social centre, thanks to its proximity to Sitges.

Arriving in **Sitges** from the east is effectively like entering through the back door. The top of the landmark church on the *punta* (promontory) is visible but it is mostly hidden, and its back is towards you. The relatively quiet, small beach of San Sebastià stretches out for little more than 90m (300ft) and at its far end is the sturdy seawall which protects the promontory.

The old town, built around the *punta*, is a delight. A narrow, cobbled street rises up to what appears to be a medieval palace, bearing the romantic name **Palau Mar i Cel** (usually contracted to Maricel), which means the 'palace of the sea and sky'. Joined above street level by walkways, and flaunting the gargoyles and galleries of a Notre Dame, the building is so tall that some of the narrow alleyways are permanently in shadow. Despite being Gothic in appearance, it was actually built in the 1920s (on the site of a 14th-century hospital) for American businessman and art collector, Charles Deering. Inside, in a room with wonderful views out to sea through floor-to-ceiling windows, the **Museu Maricel de Mar** (summer Tue–Sun 10am–2pm and 5–9pm, winter Tue–Sat 9.30am–2pm and 3.30–6.30pm, Sun 10am–3pm; charge) houses Deering's collection of paintings and *objets d'art* from around the world.

Outside the
Museu Maricel de Mar

Also on the *punta*, next door to the Museu Maricel, is the art and wrought ironwork collection of Santiago Rusiñol (1861–1931), a leading exponent of *Modernisme* who named his studio-home **Cau Ferrat** (the 'iron lair') after his work. Here, other leading sculptors and painters of the day would meet, forging the beginnings of Sitges as

Passeig Maritim in Sitges

a fashionable artists' and intellectuals' colony. Cau Ferrat holds more than just Rusiñol's splendid ironwork, however. Paintings by such masters as El Greco and Picasso, as well as beautiful ceramics and crystal are imaginatively displayed in one of Spain's most exquisite small museums.

At the very top of the hill is the **parish church**, built between the 16th and 18th centuries. It may not be an architectural gem – in fact it is quite plain by day – but its dramatic setting more than compensates for any lack of aesthetic appeal, particularly at night when it is beautifully illuminated. As you stand and look down upon the 5km (3-mile) stretch of beach and the *Passeig Maritim* (promenade) of Sitges, much of the reason for the town's appeal becomes apparent, for this is one of those increasingly rare Spanish resorts that has not fallen victim to the excesses of modern tourism.

The old town slopes inland from the church and tumbles down the narrow streets which culminate in the *Passeig*

Maritim. Antiques shops and art galleries, whitewashed houses, colourful local shops, a park where *sardanas (see page 87)* are regularly performed, enticing cafés, restaurants and lively bars can all be found here.

Another good museum in Sitges is the **Museu Romàntic**, a mansion lavishly decorated in 19th-century style and full of interesting contemporary objects, including clocks, working music boxes, and a renowned collection of dolls.

The far end of the town is quiet. Here wealthy Barcelonan families enjoy tranquillity behind lofty, trimmed hedges. It is the young, trendy Barcelonans who make Sitges such a fashionable and lively spot. Just take a walk along the *Calle 1er de Maig* (1st May) to feel the atmosphere. Since the 1960s, a sizeable and semi-permanent gay population has brought

Castellet and L'Arboç

For a half-day break from the coast between Sitges and El Vendrell, take the E15 country road from north of Vilanova i la Geltrú. This picturesque road cuts through rolling countryside and vineyards, before rising up to the hamlet of Castellet. Here, a well-preserved, sturdy medieval castle commands a marvellous view over the lovely reservoir of Panta de Foix. From the restaurant on the main road just below, you can enjoy more panoramic views while sipping an aperitif.

Continue on the same road for 3km (2 miles) to the pretty village of L'Arboç. What makes this small community special is the number of interesting buildings here. Dominating the scene is a copy of Seville's famous Giralda tower, while at the village entrance a mock castle is home to a cava winery. The most important historical structure is a Renaissance-style church, which contains a 12th-century Romanesque chapel, complete with fine, Gothic wall paintings. L'Arboç also has a renowned Modernist hospital structure, and there is a fine museum of lace in the village.

particular verve, colour and humour to Sitges. The *fiestas* here are among the most colourful outside Barcelona, with **Carnaval** being particularly outrageous. At the other end of the spectrum, however, Sitges is also known for its **Corpus Christi** celebrations.

To complete the picture, this all-around resort also offers good watersports facilities and a fine golf course. Meanwhile, at San Pere de Ribes, 3km (2 miles) north, the region's high rollers converge on the **Gran Casino de Barcelona**.

Vilanova i La Geltrú

A few kilometres along the coast, the city of **Vilanova i La Geltrú** also has an extensive sand beach, but is less developed than Sitges. Away from the beach, a bustling network of narrow streets is home to a population of some 50,000. This is a workaday Spanish town, but don't be put off by its rather unprepossessing appearance. If you don't want to venture into its maze of streets and alleyways, there are still the seafront and three good museums to explore.

The first two museums are just off the main Tarragona road. The grand *fin-de-siècle* Modernist building of the **Museu Balaguer** is clearly distinguishable from the road. It is devoted mainly to 19th- and 20th-century paintings by Catalan artists, but there are some Old Masters as well. A few metres away is a **railway museum** which will delight trainspotters of all ages. It's not so much 'hands on' as 'clamber on'. Several lovingly restored old-time locomotives are displayed in engine sheds or out in the open air.

The **Casa Papiol Museum** is tucked away in the town's backstreets. A sister building to the Museu Romàntic in Sitges, it is an 18th-century mansion re-creating Spanish noble life.

Down at the seafront (where you'll find the tourist office) is one of Catalonia's busiest **fishing ports**. Here, large international vessels jostle for space with traditional, small

Vilanova i La Geltrú – a sculpture at the port

Spanish fishing boats. Close by, the **Castillo de La Geltrú** is a much-restored 13th-century building where ancient arte-facts are exhibited alongside modern Catalan art.

A String of Resorts

The coast west of Vilanova is lined with a succession of fam-ily seaside resorts. Each is well developed (mainly with medi-um-rise apartments and hotels), and is small, neat and tidy, with long, clean golden beaches offering the usual facilities, including most watersports. The beaches of Comaruga, Cunit, Calafell and Sant Salvador are all good for swimming.

The first of these resorts is **Cubelles**, where some of the beaches have been shaped by the tide into attractive crescents – perfect for safe swimming. The village also has an impos-ing 17th-century church. Neighbouring **Cunit** also has a good beach, stretching some 3km (2 miles), although divided by breakwaters.

Next is the lengthy shore of **Calafell**, the most developed of this group of resorts. The old part is dominated by the ruins of a sturdy-looking castle perched on a hill. The town of Calafell peters out into Segur de Calafell, where there is a small marina.

With its ancient buildings, which include a medieval city gate, and a small Rambla, **El Vendrell** is the most distinctive of these coastal towns. It is also an important wine town and you will see fields of vines in the surrounding area. For sea and sand take the road for some 3km (2 miles) to the town's beach at Sant Salvador.

Finally in this small group is **Comaruga**, another well-developed and fashionable resort with big hotels to complement its comfortable villas. Known as a spa and sporting centre, it also has a small marina and a beach stretching for over 4km (2½ miles).

The N246 coast road stops at Comaruga and heads inland to pick up the busy N340 which continues east as the new coast route. This follows the Roman road, the Appian Way, and just beyond Comaruga is a reminder of those days. In the middle of the road stands a huge, triumphal arch known as the **Arc**

Pablo Casals (1876–1973)

Born in El Vendrell in 1876, the cellist, Pablo (Pau) Casals, became one of the great musicians of the 20th century (tirelessly continuing to perform well into his eighties), as well as being a champion of human rights and a staunch advocate of Catalan independence.

If you want to learn more about him, go along to the beach quarter of El Vendrell, Sant Salvador, where his old summer house is open to the public. In addition to musical memorabilia, the house holds a fine collection of Catalan art. Concerts are held periodically at the auditorium opposite.

de Berà. It's as tall as a three-storey building and has stood here since the 2nd century. Cars used to drive through it, but increased traffic dictates that they now go around it. Look out for the turn-off to **Roc Sant Gaietà**; the eponymous rock on which the village is built overlooks an attractive, unspoiled cove.

Torredembarra, by contrast, is a busier resort with a broad, long beach. The town, however, has been virtually untouched and has a very solid church and a fine, old castle in an endearing state of decay.

Altafulla

Altafulla

Next door is **Altafulla**, arguably the prettiest settlement between Tarragona and Sitges. This picturesque town of well-preserved pink, stone houses, many of which date from the 18th century, climbs steeply up narrow streets, towards the church and the 11th-century castle. En route is the town's modern art museum, housed in an historic property.

Altafulla has a reasonable beach of the same name and close by is the excellent beach of **Tamarit**. A narrow track leads off the main road, wending through vegetable fields and a campsite, until it comes to the dramatic cliff-top Castle of Tamarit (not open to the public), built in the 11th century to defend the coast against the Moors. Below it you'll find the beach.

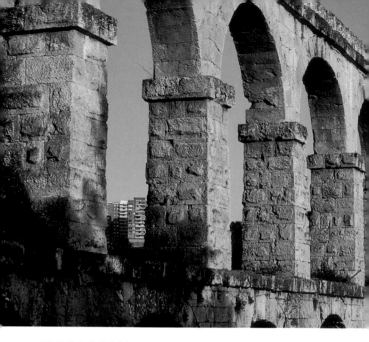

TARRAGONA

Tarragona is best entered from the east along the old Vía Augusta, where ancient Roman roadside monuments whet the appetite for the historic city that is to come.

Continuing on our journey from the east, just off the main road is **El Médol**, the stone quarry which provided the raw materials for several of the Roman structures in Tarragona. The vertical quarry walls plunge down to a monolith known as **L'Agulla del Médol** (the Needle of Médol). Carved from the original rock, it was deliberately worked to indicate the depth of the excavations. Note the type of stone here; you

The Pont del Diable

will see it later in a more polished state in the buildings of Tarragona.

Just a little further on, and at the very edge of the road, is the **Torre de los Escipiones** (Tower of the Scipios – two brothers who were important protagonists in early Roman military campaigns in Hispania). Little can be said with certainty about this immense, square funerary tower, but the figures still visible on the front of the monument are thought to represent Atis, an Eastern god of the funerary cult. The tower is probably a tomb and certainly at one time had a pyramidal top. Unfortunately the elements and other vagaries of time have taken their toll on its exterior.

Tarragona's most impressive Roman monument lies some 4km (2½ miles) north of the centre of town, off the N240 Lleida (Lérida) road. If you thought that they didn't come much bigger than the towering Arc de Berà (see page 42) then you'd be wrong.

The **Pont del Diable** (the Devil's Bridge) is one of the greatest Roman structures still standing in Spain. A perfectly preserved double-decker aqueduct, it spans 217m (712ft), and has a total of 11 lower-storey and 25 upper-storey arches, the highest of which rise up to 27m (88ft) from the ground. It was built during the 1st century as part of a complex network of canals that supplied Tarragona with water, and even today remains a tribute to the engineers of the day. Not only is the stonework in superb condition, but in places the original watercourse is still intact. The structure is also known as the aqueduct of 'Les Ferreres', which refers to the rusty, red water it carried over its arches.

The best viewpoint is from above, off the A7 motorway, where sightseeing coaches pull over. If you want to see the aqueduct up close, access is not easy. Look for a very narrow turning roughly 0.5km (¼ mile) south (Tarragona side) of the Restaurant Pont del Diable (you may well have to double back on yourself). It is unmarked, but there is a dilapidated entrance of sorts (take care when exiting from the busy main road). It is then a 10-minute walk to the bottom of the overgrown valley that the aqueduct spans (although it is not in sight for most of the walk).

From the east, the Vía Augusta runs into the **Rambla Vella** (Old Rambla), which neatly divides the town in half. To the north is the old walled city, while parallel and to the south is the **Rambla Nova** (New Rambla) and the newer part of town. Before heading for the sights, relax at a café on the Rambla Nova and visit the very helpful tourist office, which will supply you with town maps and any other details you require.

Blood of Christ

If you've ever wondered where the wine that is used to celebrate Holy Communion comes from, the answer may well be Tarragona.

De Muller, the city's largest and most prestigious wine concern, have been specialist suppliers of altar wine for generations. Exporting organically produced red wine all over the world, they have been suppliers to the Vatican and many popes. In keeping with the changing taste of the market as a whole, altar wines have become less sweet in recent years.

Passeig Arqueològic

Roman Tarragona

The Romans landed in Tarragona (they called it Tarraco) in the 3rd century BC and rapidly established it as an important military and political headquarters. It grew to a population of 30,000, coined its own money and by 27BC was the capital of Hispania Citerior (later Tarraconensis), the largest Roman province in Spain. During the Roman occupation, a number of emperors lived here, including Augustus and Hadrian. In 2000, the **Archaeological Ensemble of Tarraco** was declared a Unesco World Heritage Site.

The best place to start getting acquainted with ancient Tarraco is the Passeig Arqueològic (Archaeological Promenade) which follows the top of the old **city walls** just north of the Rambla Vella. The walls were built by the Romans immediately on their arrival. They rise up to 12m (39ft) high and in places are up to 6m (19ft) wide. This feat of engineering had a head start, however, since the initial settlers (peoples from the eastern Mediterranean) had somehow already placed in position titanic blocks, each weighing up to 35 tonnes, which the Romans promptly used as foundation stones.

The walk incorporates three solid Roman towers, a fine statue of the Emperor Augustus (presented by Mussolini), attractive gardens, and fine views. Don't be misled, however, into thinking the 'Greek Theatre' just down the hill is from antiquity; it's a modern municipal auditorium, built in 1970.

The British have also left their mark on the fortifications, their forces having positioned the outer walls in 1707 to secure the city during the War of Succession. The walk actually finishes outside the walls, but don't worry, to get back inside just keep the walls to your right and walk the short distance to the **Portal de Sant Antoni**. The ornamentation is 18th century, but the gate is much older.

You are now entering a labyrinthine **medieval city**, with flowerpots balanced on iron balconies, and canaries in cages on the walls. You might also see patriotic red- and yellow-striped Catalan flags draped from verandah railings.

If you can resist wandering at random through this fascinating part of town, stick to the Via Granada until you reach the Plaça del Rei (King's Square). The **Museu Arqueològic** (summer Tue–Sat 9.30am–8.30pm, Sun 10am–2pm, winter Tue–Sat 9.30am–1.30pm and 3.30–7pm, Sun 10am–2pm; charge) here is a modern, well-designed exhibition of delicate mosaics and Roman and Spanish artefacts.

Pretori Romà

The ancient, roughly hewn, tall, golden building adjacent to the museum is known as the **Pretori Romà** (Roman Prætorium; summer Tue–Sat 10am–9pm, Sun 9am–3pm, winter Tue–Sat 9am–7pm, Sun 10am–3pm; charge), and is thought to have been part of the complex of original provincial administration buildings. During this period it also acquired the name of Castell de Pilate (Pilate's Castle), since it was traditionally known as the birthplace of Pontius Pilate. Pilate's father was prætor here before moving to Judea, where his son was to follow in his footsteps. The Emperor Augustus is also believed to have used the building as a palace, and so too did the medieval Aragonese kings, whence its other name, Castell del Rei (Kings' Castle). It is certainly Roman in origin, though much restored in the Middle Ages, and it now houses the **Museum of Roman Artefacts**.

The contrast between the ancient, atmospheric shell of the building and the stylish, modern exhibition of artifacts telling the story of old Tarragona (captions in Spanish only) works well. Look out for the Sarcophagus of Hippolytus, recovered from the sea in 1948. At the lowest level you can walk a short way along a tunnel which linked the castle with the Roman **circus** (part of which was on the site where the Plaça de la Font now stands) and acted as supporting vaults for the circus tiers. Just next door to the Pretori Romà are further remains of the circus.

Amphitheatre
Walking from here towards the sea brings you to the hillside ruins of the Roman **amphitheatre**. Gladiators once fought here, and on this site, in AD259, the first Christians

The Roman amphitheatre

Remnants of the forum

on the peninsula were martyred by fire. A church, dedicated to their memory, was built within the amphitheatre, but only its ruins remain.

Three other important ancient sites, situated beyond the city walls, should also be mentioned before we turn again to medieval Tarragona.

Near the colourful central market on Carrer Lleida are the remains of Tarragona's local **forum** (the city's provincial forum was set inside the city walls). Not much is left now: a few isolated columns and arches bear testimony to the once arcaded square which in Roman times would have been filled with court rooms, temples, shops and other buildings.

The second site dates from towards the end of the Roman period, and is located on the western edge of the city centre. The **Necròpolis i Museu Paleocristià** (Necropolis and Paleo-Christian Museum; summer Tue–Sat 10am–1.30pm and 4–7pm, Sun 10am–2pm, winter Tue–Sat 9.30am–1.30pm and 3–5.30pm, Sun 10am–2pm; charge) is on the site of a cemetery for Tarragona's early Christians, and comprises a series of covered excavations. More than 2,000 graves have been unearthed here, and a museum displays the best of the finds. Naturally, it's not the cheeriest of places, but there are some good pieces in the museum, including fine sarcophagi. Perhaps best of all is the colourful 4th-century

Optimus Sepulchral Mosaic, regarded as a masterpiece of early Christian art. Note too the unusual ivory doll which holds pride of place in an illuminated case. Fully articulated, it was found in a child's grave and dates from the 3rd century.

If you'd like to learn more about late Roman/early Christian ways of life and death, head north for 5km

(3 miles) to Constanti, and in the village of **Centcelles** you will find a 4th-century villa and mausoleum. The mosaics on the cupola represent a deer hunt, the four seasons, and biblical stories, including Daniel in the Lion's Den and Jonah and the Whale. This may have been intended as the last resting place for Emperor Constans, who died in AD350, and indeed some authorities claim that he is actually buried here.

Medieval Tarragona

To return to the old city, re-enter by the side of the Pretori, and from the Plaça del Rei take the Vía Santa Anna. To the left is the **Museu d'Art Modern**, where, in a fine city mansion, the shock of the new contrasts well with the grace of the old.

To the right is Passage Angels, which leads into the medieval **Barrí Jueu** (Jewish Quarter), still proud owner of some of its original Gothic arches. At the end of Santa Anna are some more Roman remains – the walls of the city's Provincial Forum.

Turn left into La Mercería (Haberdasher's Street), which during the Middle Ages was the market area and which still retains its 14th-century arcades. On Sunday morning the clock is turned back and the area hosts an antiques market.

A little further on are the steps up to medieval Tarragona's pride and joy – the Romanesque and Gothic **Catedral** (Tue–Sat summer 10am–7pm, Nov–Mar 10am–2pm, rest of the year 10am–5pm), built between 1171 and 1331 on Tarragona's highest point, where the Romans had erected a temple to Jupiter. From the front it is rather disappointing, appearing somewhat cramped, with its front towers severely truncated. It is difficult to estimate its size from this angle, but the great Gothic doorway and one of Europe's largest rose windows give an indication. It is actually the largest cathedral in Catalonia, a region which takes its religious architecture very seriously.

Follow the arrows to the tourist entrance round to the left

The Cathedral

and you reach the **cloister**, from where the importance of this great building becomes more apparent. Constructed in the 12th and 13th centuries, the cloister is an attraction in its own right. Similar to those of the great local Cistercian monasteries, it is large (measuring some 46m/150ft down each side), airy, and incorporates a pretty garden. Notice the sculptural detail of the capitals around the cloister. The most famous is the relief known as the **Procession of the Rats**, which depicts the rodents conducting a cat's funeral (ask in the museum if you have any difficulty in locating it).

Built into the west gallery is another unexpected feature – a Muslim monument of marble. The date of this shrine is AD960, and it is thought to have arrived here as a battle trophy.

Sculpture detail

The overall effect, looking up to the vaulted ceiling, is one of austere majesty. This is regarded as one of Spain's finest cathedrals of this period. The **main altarpiece**, carved in alabaster by the 15th-century Catalan master, Pere Johan, shows excellent lifelike detail. It is dedicated to Santa Tecla, the local patron saint, who is said to have been converted to Christianity by St Paul, who actually preached in Tarragona. To the right of the altar, look out for the sculpted tomb of Prince Juan de Aragón, an archbishop of the city who died in 1334.

In total there are 19 chapels in the cathedral, ranging in style from high medieval art to 19th-century kitsch. The best are those dedicated to: Nostra Senyora de Montserrat of the 15th century; Santa María dels Sastres (of the tailors) of the 14th century; and Santa Tecla of the 18th century.

The cathedral's **Museu Diocesà** has a fine collection of ecclesiastical art and ancient objects, including many impressive Flemish tapestries. These are all well lit and displayed in several rooms around the cloister.

Outside, the narrow, cobbled streets surrounding the cathedral have changed little since the Middle Ages. It's worth walking all the way around the cathedral to view it from different angles. Just before you return to the front square, you will see the **Antic Hospital** (Old Hospital) which was constructed between the 12th and 14th centuries and is now a local government office.

Descend the steps from the cathedral square and about 100m to your left, along Carrer Major, is Carrer de la Nau, known for its antiques shops. To the right is Vía Cavallers and the **Casa Museu Castellarnau** (summer Tue–Sat 9am–9pm, Sun 9am–3pm, winter Tue–Sat 9am–7pm, Sun 10am–3pm). The Castellarnaus were a noble, city-dwelling family whose 18th–19th-century mansion has recently been renovated with sumptuous period fittings and a small museum.

Modern Tarragona

Tarragona is capital of the 9,842-sq-km (3,800-sq-mile) province of the same name, and with a population of more than 130,000, it is a big town in most respects. Surprisingly,

Along the Rambla Nova

in view of its historical legacy and the number of good beaches literally on its doorstep, it is only just beginning to wake up to the potential of tourism.

Stroll along the **Rambla Nova** to feel the pulse of the city. It's not the same as the bustling Rambla of Barcelona, but it does have the confident air of a city endowed with a rich past and a prosperous present. While walking along the Rambla, note the Modernist flourishes on buildings. Past the statue of Admiral Roger de Lauria, a swashbuckling 13th-century hero, is the clifftop viewing point known as the **Balcó del Mediterrani** (Balcony of the Mediterranean).

Down to the left is the long, golden strip of the **Platja del Miracle**. Follow the coast road east and you'll find more pretty coves and beaches. Watersports tuition is available at Platja Llarga and hire equipment at Platja de la Savinosa, Platja de la Móra and Platja de l'Arrabassada. The last is probably the best beach, but at most times of year all offer excellent possibilities for delightful uncrowded swimming and sunbathing.

The Port

From the Balcó del Mediterrani you can also look down on the **port** of Tarragona. This is one of the three largest commercial ports in Spain, and one of the busiest in the whole Mediterranean. The adjacent fishing port is well worth a visit. Its waterfront district is unaccountably known as El Serrall, meaning 'the harem'. Yachts are moored on the seaward side of the harbour wall, at the impressive new International Marina Tarraco.

Finest fish

Away from the boats, the harbour and old backstreets of El Serrall are also worth exploring for the area's fish restaurants. Some of Tarragona's finest seafood is served here, often in plain surroundings.

Boats hauled up at Salou

TARRAGONA TO THE EBRO DELTA

While the coast to the east of Tarragona offers good beaches, historical monuments and several attractive settlements, the strip immediately to the west is largely given over to industry.

The first resort, **Pineda de Mar**, is an overspill from Salou and offers a fine 3km (2-mile) beach with most facilities. Pineda is particularly popular with young people, mostly due to the waterpark, Acquapark *(see page 92)*, and the adjacent fashionable nightspot.

Salou

Salou has been a major cosmopolitan resort for over 20 years, and a well-ordered, no-frills playground for holidaymakers on a budget. It has two long, sandy beaches, stretching for over 1.5km (1 mile), named Llevant/Levante ('sunrise') to the east and Ponente/Poniente ('sunset') to the west.

Llevant, the livelier of the two, is bordered by a palm-shaded promenade dotted with benches and colourful flower arrangements. The east end of the beach is particularly geared to entertainment. Street stalls sell souvenirs, cafés serve traditional tea, and restaurants dish out German, Dutch and British food, while bars compete to offer the highest number of satellite-television channels. In the early evening, the crowds gather to watch the town's **illuminated fountain**. It was designed by Buigas (famous for his dancing fountains in Barcelona) and has become a symbol of Salou.

Just to the east of Platja Llevant is the relatively small, 200m (650ft) cove of **Platja de Capellans**. Pine trees and tall cliffs help to make this an attractive spot, but it can get very crowded.

The far end, east of Llevant beach, offers Salou's permanent funfair, good shopping and a few up-market hotels. At the corner of the promenade and Carrer Barcelona, look out for the Casa Bonet, a beautiful, Modernist mansion designed in 1918–19 by the renowned architect Domènec Sugranyes, who took over the work on Gaudí's unfinished Sagrada Família cathedral in Barcelona *(see page 31)*.

Just inland from the front (behind the railway station) is the town's only major historical structure. The very solid **Torre Vella** (Old Tower) was built during the 16th century as a form of protection against Algerian and Turkish pirates. It now houses a museum of modern art.

Salou's greatest attraction is the **Port Aventura** theme park, a 10-minute

Salou's Paseo Jaime I

El Conquistador

Although Salou is not famous for its historical associations, its Llevant beach was in fact the embarkation point for the Armada of King Jaume I in 1229. His forces wrested Majorca from Moorish control, thus adding another territory to the kingdom of Catalonia and earning the king the nickname El Conquistador (Conqueror). Jaume is commemorated by a large, modern monument on the promenade which also bears his name.

ride from town. Water rides, rollercoasters and other amusements complement reproductions of villages from various parts of the world, including Mexico, China and Polynesia.

Platja Ponent has a pleasant promenade and is a long and busy beach (though compared with Llevant it can seem quite quiet). This merges into the residential suburb of Vilafortuny which in turn drifts into Cambrils. Before you get to Cambrils proper, however, there are fine pine-shaded beaches on which to relax.

Cambrils

Cambrils is an attractive fishing port-turned-resort. It has a long seafront, and much of its charm stems from the large fleet of *bous* – small fishing boats which carry oversized lamps for night duty – at anchor here. The reliable catch has helped turn Cambrils into a Catalan gourmet town. Its waterfront has more good restaurants than many a metropolis (almost twice as many as Tarragona, for example) and attracts connoisseurs of good food from all over the region.

Pleasure boats run regularly between Salou and Cambrils, and also up and down the coast on excursions to L'Ametlla de Mar and Tarragona, as well as to the Sunday market at L'Hospitalet de l'Infant.

Set back from the waterfront at Cambrils is the town centre – small but lively, with old, unspoiled streets and a fine indoor market. On the main road, heading south out of town, look out for the fine, old **Torre de l'Ermita** (Hermitage Tower), which is next door to the hermitage/church of Mare de Déu del Camí. The tower houses a small museum.

Cambrils is the last major resort on the Costa Dorada. Southwest of here, the coast becomes mostly quiet and undeveloped. There are several minor resorts, however, the first of which is the pleasant beach of **Miami Platja**.

Just next door, **L'Hospitalet de l'Infant** (the Hospice of the Prince) is also a small beach resort occupying an attractive setting in a large bay backed by hills. Its name is derived from a 14th-century hospice for pilgrims, whose ruins can still be seen today.

A cat among the nets at Cambrils

L'Ametlla de Mar

A little further along the coast, past the startling red-and-white nuclear power station of Vandellós, lies **L'Ametlla de Mar**, a quiet, very old-fashioned fishing village which is well worth a visit. Watch the boats coming in with the catch, or the fishermen unravelling twisted nets on the quay, disentangling tiny *langostinos* (prawns). With four beaches close by, L'Ametlla has also become something of a tourist centre.

Just past the small port of **L'Ampolla**, the coastline changes dramatically. Out go the hills and beaches and in their place come great, flat tracts of land. In spring they become waterlogged and give off a blue-green colour; in summer they turn gold when filled with ears of rice, or green with vegetable crops; and in winter they return to bare brown earth.

Ebro Delta

This is the **Ebro Delta**, the largest wetlands in Catalonia and, after France's famous Carmague, the most important aquatic environment in the western Mediterranean. The Delta was created from mud washed down the River Ebro all the way from Zaragoza. The river continues to throw up

Birdwatching in the Ebro Delta

The second-largest wetland area in western Europe after the Carmargue in southern France, the Ebro Delta is both a major breeding ground for waterfowl, waders and seabirds, and an important resting site for winter migrants. The total bird population varies seasonally between 50,000 and 100,000, and includes 60 percent of all species found in Europe. The best months to visit are October and November after the rice harvest, when the fields remain flooded attracting migrants to stop and feed. The most common species are coots, ducks (including shoveler, wigeon, shelduck, gadwall, teal and pochard) and waders, such as the great crested grebe, black-winged stilt and avocet. Among the larger and more interesting birds to be seen are the cattle egret, night heron, squacco heron, purple heron and flamingo. There are lookout towers at various strategic locations but many birds can be seen – with binoculars – from the roads and footpaths.

Sand dunes on the Ebro Delta at Platja Riumar

new land and the Delta expands some 10m (33ft) into the sea each year. It now covers an area of more than 320 sq km (123 sq miles), of which 7,690 hectares (19,000 acres), or just under 25 percent of the total area, have been set aside as a protected Natural Park.

The Ebro Delta is a rich agricultural district famous for its rice, though many other fruit and vegetable crops also flourish in the rich soil.

There aren't many roads in this quiet part of the world, but it's still quite possible to get lost, so take care. Follow the road to **Deltebre** (formerly named La Cava) where there is a tourist office. In addition to supplying general information and maps, the office will also be able to advise you on the best places for birdwatching *(see page 60)*. Inquire about boat excursions which leave from Deltebre (or you can hire a boat from Amposta). You'll need the best part of a day, perhaps more, to explore both north and south of the Delta.

Rice farming in the Ebro

If time is limited, stick to the south. Take the old-fashioned *transbordador* (car-ferry, the only way across the Ebro) at **Sant Jaume d'Enveja**, and head south to the long and rather desolate ocean-like beaches of Platja dels Eucaliptus and Platja del Trabucador. Due south, the Peninsula dels Alfacs is part of the Natural Park, and is off limits to cars.

Unless you're an ornithologist, the principal beauty of the Ebro is its peace, calm and wide-open space. Like Florida's Everglades, there is no spectacular scenery here, but there are vignettes of a slower, almost vanished way of life: small, thatched, white-washed houses; ramshackle smallholders' huts; rice workers sowing and reaping, and villagers cycling languorously between the paddies. Look out too for horses drawing plough-like contraptions which winnow the chaff from the grain on concrete aprons.

When visiting the Delta in spring, summer or early autumn, you should bring mosquito repellent with you; they are the most widespread and characteristic insect of the Delta.

Sant Carles de la Ràpita

Sant Carles de la Ràpita, with a population of 14,000, is the main town of the Delta, though it is totally unlike any of the tiny agricultural settlements here. Its large, natural harbour serves a prosperous fishing fleet and ship-building industry. What really distinguishes the town, however, is its gigantic main square. It is so enormous for such a small town that there aren't enough public buildings, shops and offices to fill its perimeter (many of the buildings are private houses). It was the brainchild of Charles III, who envisaged Sant Carles as a port of great significance. The project died with him in 1788, but the great melancholy square remains.

Amposta

South of Sant Carles is the River Alcanar and the border with the Costa del Azahar. Turn north instead towards Amposta and Tortosa. **Amposta**, a town of some 20,000 inhabitants, is located on the south bank of the Ebro. The compact centre includes some notable examples of *Modernisme*, and there's a museum about the Delta. The river is spanned by an impressive suspension bridge dating from 1921.

Amposta, with its hallmark suspension bridge

Tortosa

Tortosa held a key strategic role for many centuries as the last major town before the sea, guarding the Ebro River which rises in the north of Spain. The elaborate fortress at the top of the town was built by the Moors, who held out at length here during the 1148 Reconquest. Under the Aragonese kings, it became a royal residence known as the Castle of San Juan. Today it is better known by its Arabic name, **La Suda**, and houses a *parador* (state-owned hotel). It's a long and steep walk up, so if you would prefer to drive, follow the river a little way out of town and then backtrack up the hill. It's well worth the climb, as this is the only vantage point from where you can take in the whole city, and particularly the cathedral.

From the ground, the **cathedral** is tightly hemmed in, but viewed from on high, it is a much more impressive sight. Built between the 14th and 16th centuries, it's a fine example of Catalan Gothic architecture. Inside, do not miss the 14th-century triptych or the two 15th-century carved stone pulpits.

From La Suda, it is also easy to see the remains of the old **city walls**.

Battle of the Ebro

Due to its strategically important location, the town of Tortosa has witnessed much bloodshed in the course of its long history, but no carnage so terrible as the Battle of the Ebro in 1938. This was one of the worst conflicts of the Spanish Civil War, resulting in an overwhelming victory for Franco's Nationalists, and the loss of 20,000 lives (estimates of casualties vary enormously). A monument to those who fell, in the form of a striking, modern structure, rises arrow-like from a concrete island in the middle of the Ebro.

Picturesque Peñíscola

Beyond the Ebro

A trip to the northern Costa del Azahar is worth the drive
south from the Tarragona provincial border. The 'Orange Blos-
som Coast', stretching for 112km (70 miles), is endowed with
beaches and olive and citrus groves after which it is named.

Peñíscola lies 122km (75 miles) from Tarragona. The picturesque old town, crowned by a medieval castle, sits on a
rocky promontory. The **castle**, built by the Knights Templar
on the ruins of a Moorish fortress, has two claims to fame:
Pope Benedict XIII found asylum here after being dismissed
from his position until his death in 1423; and it featured in
the film *El Cid*, starring Charlton Heston. There's a museum and great sea views from the restored ramparts.

Stretching northwards from the promontory, parallel to
the busy new town, is Peñíscola's star attraction – a 5km (3-
mile) long sandy beach lapped by clean, calm waters. Be
warned that it gets very crowded in summer.

INLAND EXCURSIONS

Montserrat

For 700 years, pilgrims have been climbing the mighty rock formation to reach the **Monastery of Montserrat**. Now that donkeys and foot power have been replaced by cable-cars and coaches, about a million people every year make the trip to the spiritual heart of Catalonia.

There have been hermitages here since medieval times, possibly to escape the Moorish invasion. One such hermitage was enlarged to become a Benedictine monastery, and in the 12th century it became the repository of a small, brown statue of the Virgin Mary, **La Moreneta** (the Little Dark Madonna). Legend has it that statue was made by St Luke and brought to Barcelona by St Peter. La Moreneta was subsequently adopted as the patron saint of Catalonia, and pilgrims have come to worship her ever since.

The original monastery was destroyed in 1808 by Napoleon's troops, and the present one dates from 1874. This is very much a living, working monastery and public entrance is only permitted to the basilica. A highlight of the visit is the famous **Escolania choir**, a children's choir founded in the 13th century, which sings angelically at 1pm and 6.45pm Monday to Thursday, 1pm on Friday and noon on Sunday.

The monastery also houses a good **museum**, with works of art by such masters as El Greco, Picasso and Caravaggio,

and a fine collection of modern Catalan paintings and archaeological treasures from the biblical Orient, including Egyptian mummies. Look out for the beautiful, Gothic cloistered section next door.

Complaints are frequently voiced about the commercialisation of the monastery grounds, and souvenir stalls do proliferate alongside restaurants and a hotel. But even if the aesthetics of such development may be questionable, the monastery's magnificent setting in beautiful protected **mountain parkland** provides inspiration to the most wooden of hearts.

Above: the Monastery of Montserrat

You can get here by car or rack railway, but the best approach is by **cable-car**. The terminal is on the C1411 Barcelona–Manresa road. Join the queue, then it's up and away, over 1,000m (3,300ft) to the mountain top, probably breaking through the clouds en route. The view of the mountains, which certainly live up to their name (*montserrat* means 'serrated-' or 'saw-toothed mountain') is magical.

Poblet

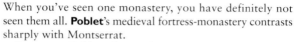

When you've seen one monastery, you have definitely not seen them all. **Poblet**'s medieval fortress-monastery contrasts sharply with Montserrat.

For a start, Poblet (about 45km/28 miles from Tarragona) usually seems to be less crowded, even though it is the largest and best-preserved Cistercian monastery in Europe. While Montserrat clings to its granite eyrie, Poblet sprawls across a green open plateau amid fertile hillsides; and while both have in times past been ruthlessly plundered, Montserrat today is only a structural replica of its true former glory, whereas Poblet is as close to its original medieval state as is possible.

Heavenly Walks

If you want to escape the crowds at Montserrat, this pristine area is a protected Natural Park and a walker's paradise. There are four main walks, all well signposted. One of these, Santa Cova (30 minutes), leads to the holy cave where La Moreneta was supposedly discovered. The other three lead to hermitages: Sant Joan (15–20 minutes from the top of the funicular terminal); Sant Miquel (30 minutes); and Sant Jeroni (1 hour 30 minutes). The views on all the walks are spectacular.

Funiculars climb up the steep hillsides to the start of the walks to Sant Joan and Santa Cova. Although rather expensive, they are well worth the money in terms of breath saved.

The monastery was founded in 1151 by the Count of Barcelona, Ramón Berenguer IV, as a gesture of thanks for the reconquest of Catalonia from the Moors. Royal patronage down the ages brought Poblet fame and fortune, as well as historical importance.

The ultimate accolade of royal pantheon (burial place) was bestowed by Peter the Ceremonious during the 14th century. He and seven other kings of Aragon are interred here in unique **tombs** which are suspended on low arches in the cross vault of the church. Only fragments of the original tomb sculptures have been preserved, so the carvings you see today are skilled reproductions.

The monastery of Poblet

As you enter the grounds, the **front** of the monastery is a majestic sight. Its towers, belfries, lanterns and walls are as imposing as those of any castle. Since Poblet is still a working monastery, visitors are not allowed to wander at will. A guided tour takes you past the vaulted wine cellars, the library, chapterhouse, the refectory, and into the impressive Gothic-Romanesque church. It's big and airy, and in accordance with the Cistercian way of life, shuns any kind of ornamentation.

However, perhaps the real appreciation of the monastic mood comes in the form of the **cloister**. This too is large and atmospheric, with four brooding poplars and a rose garden. Only the trickle of water and birdsong disturbs the serenity. At one time around 200 monks lived and worked here; today there are around 30.

Santes Creus

About 40km (25 miles) from Poblet, and 36km (22 miles) from Tarragona, another great **monastery** sprawls among the vineyards. Santes Creus (Holy Crosses), a Cistercian foundation, was established just six years after Poblet, in 1157. Comparisons with Poblet are obvious. Santes Creus is much smaller and less grand, but even from within the shadow of its bigger and more famous neighbour, it is still an architectural masterpiece.

The **cloisters** are once again a highlight (two here). The Great Cloister is classic Catalan Gothic, dating from the 14th

The monastery of Santes Creus

century, and includes some uncharacteristically light-hearted touches. Look out for heraldic designs, animals and humorous faces carved on the arches and walls. The Infirmary cloister is plain and very peaceful.

There is also a superb vaulted **chapterhouse** with tombs of 16th-century abbots set into the floor and, upstairs, a spacious **dormitory** with a large timber-arched roof.

Cloisters at Santes Creus

Santes Creus was the royal resting place before the honour passed to Poblet, and two kings are buried here. Peter the Great (*Pere II* or *Pedro el Grande* who died in 1285) lies in a splendid **Gothic tabernacle** and close by is the beautifully sculpted tomb of Peter's son, James the Just, who died in 1327. Santes Creus also reveals its regal connections in the remains of the living quarters – the **Royal Palace**, built on the orders of Peter II. These surround a perfect 14th-century patio of delicate arches and a lovely staircase.

The monastery, disbanded in 1835, and then pillaged, was never re-established. Instead, it became a parish church and was recently taken over by the state as a museum.

Vilafranca del Penedés

The town of **Vilafranca del Penedés** is situated on a fertile plain, midway between Barcelona and Tarragona. Over the past two centuries, Vilafranca has literally grown its own success story, helping the Penedés become one of the best-known wine regions.

There are no *bodegas* to visit in the centre of town, but you will find one of Spain's very best wine museums, the **Vinseum** (June–Aug Tue–Sat 10am–7pm, Sun 10am–2pm, Sept–May Tue–Sat 10am–2pm and 4–7pm, Sun 10am–2pm; charge) – and you don't have to be a connoisseur to appreciate the exhibits. Dioramas illustrate wine through the ages and you can see huge, wooden **wine presses** used to crush grapes when the Romans were in the province. Another hall displays the glass bottles and jugs which have quenched centuries of thirst, and there is even an art gallery devoted to the noble vine.

The wine museum shares its quarters with the **Museu de Vilafranca**, which is devoted to geology, archaeology, natural history and Catalan religious art. Formerly a medieval palace of the counts of Barcelona and the kings of Aragon, the building is an attraction in its own right. Look out from the third-floor windows and you will be able to

Harvest time near Vilafranca del Penedés

see a monument to another of Vilafranca del Penedés' passions – a five-storey human pyramid team of *castellers* (*see page 86*).

Vilafranca's leafy Rambla and old town are full of character, particularly on Saturday when it hosts one of the region's liveliest general **markets**. Visit the splendid **Basílica de Santa María**, the adjacent **Palau Baltà** and the church of **Sant Francesc**, which is famous for its Catalan Gothic treasures.

Wines and cavas for sale

Pick up a map from the helpful tourist office in the town hall and ask them about visits to nearby vineyards. The **Torres vineyard**, which lies a short distance out of town, is king of the Catalan labels, and one of the world's great wine producers. Torres is known for its technical innovation and all its wines are made in temperature-controlled stainless-steel vats. The tour reflects this, and traditionalists are likely to feel that such methods take the romance out of the vine. If that's the case, you may well find the tours at **Sant Sadurní d'Anoia** (12km/7 miles to the northeast) more interesting.

Sant Sadurní is famous as the centre of production of the sparkling cava, and several **cava houses** are open to visitors. Here you descend to deep cellars where the wine is stored at a constant temperature, and the method of manufacture (identical to that for Champagne) is explained. The tour at **Freixenet** (pronounced fre-JER-nay with a soft 'j' as in the French *je*) is recommended. **Cordoníu** also puts on a good tour and is renowned for its interesting Modernist buildings.

The covered market in Reus

Reus and Montblanc

Reus is the place which every charter tourist flies into, yet few return to properly explore; which is a shame, because this is a bustling and provincial centre with plenty of charm.

The centre is the **Plaza de Mercadal**, an elegant square, porticoed on one side and little changed (traffic aside) since the 19th century. Reus' most famous son was Antoni Gaudí, born here in 1852, but surprisingly he has left no marks of any significance in his hometown. Instead the task was left to his followers. The ornate **Casa de Navàs** on the Plaza Mercadal is the town's finest Modernist building.

Reus's most handsome buildings are grouped together on the *Ruta del Modernismo* (Modernist Trail). The tourist office will provide you with a leaflet and map, and will also arrange for you to see inside some of the houses that are normally closed to the public. On your way, you may want to see the 16th-century church of Saut Pere or visit the Museu Comarcal, featuring sculpture and architecture. The town is at its best on a Monday, which is **market day**. Nuts and dried fruit gathered from the countryside are local specialities.

Montblanc lies 25km (15 miles) northeast of Reus and is the capital of its province. There any similarity ends, for this is a compact **walled town**, where many of the monuments date from the 14th century.

Go to the **Plaça Major** and look in the lobby of the town hall. The building dates from the 13th century, though its present front is 400–500 years younger. Opposite the town hall, the building with the balcony is known as the **Casal dels Desclergue**. This is the former residence of a *veguer*, the king's representative in the 16th century, when Montblanc was one of the most important towns in Catalonia. The 13th-century **Palau Reial** (Royal Palace) is just a few metres away, but is much altered from its original state.

The town's major monument is the Gothic church of **Santa María la Major** (follow the street opposite Casal dels Desclergue). But it's fun just to wander in Montblanc, spotting vestiges of the ancient past in old buildings, and of the more recent past in old-fashioned shop windows.

There are two **museums** in the walled town. The Museu Comarcal de la Conca de Barberà is in the 18th-century Casal dels Jova, and the Museu Marés (painting and sculpture) is in the church of Santa Marçal. Two **churches** worth a look are Sant Miquel and Sant Francesc, both 13th-century,

Cloisters in Montblanc

and both home, at different times, to the medieval *Corts Catalanes* (Catalan Parliament).

Espluga de Francolí, 10km (6 miles) to the north, is worth a visit for its **Museu de Vida Rural** (Rural Life Museum). This display of life as it was in the mainly agricultural Conca de Barberà province, covers four floors of an 18th-century house and is bright and cheery.

Samá Park and Escornalbou

As you head north from Cambrils on the road to Montbrió del Camp, there is a curious sight at the junction with the road to Reus and Vinyols. On top of a small mountain stump, inset with viewing balconies, is a **medieval castle tower**. Turn right down this road; the entrance to **Samá Park** is on the left (daily, summer 10am–9pm, winter 10am–5pm, closing times vary in winter, closed on rainy or windy days; charge).

This fantasy park, begun in 1881, was the brainchild of Don Salvador Samá Torrens, a Cuban heir who wanted to bring some of the atmosphere of the lost Spanish colony to the Costa Dorada. Its walled grounds cover 14 hectares (35 acres) and contain a lake, waterfalls, ornate fountains and abundant **exotic flora**, including yuccas, banana and mandarin trees, Indian nettle trees, various palms and a 20m (66ft) -high Mexican species which grows and lives with its roots in water. It is a popular place with just about everybody: children tackle the look-out towers, the 'pirate cave' and the play area; newlyweds come here to pose for

Peacock at Samá Park

Castell d'Escornalbou

romantic photographs *à deux*; and the Cambrils locals enjoy a relaxing Sunday stroll.

Continue east to Montbrió del Camp and Riudecanyes and follow the signs to the **Monestir/Castell d'Escornalbou**. The ancient monastery and castle sit high on top of a hill, which ascends steeply to a height of over 640m (2,100ft).

The monastery, built between the 13th and 15th centuries, was destroyed in 1835 and much of it is now a romantic ruin. The solid Romanesque **church** has been well restored, however, and the castle-residence exhibits pottery, furniture and archaeological finds. A cloister wall has been rebuilt, and today the distant countryside can be seen through its arches.

On a clear, sunny day, the **views** from here are marvellous, and you can enjoy a walk along the old 'monks' path'. On a cool and misty day, however, it's atmosphere becomes entirely different – a brooding, lonely sort of spot – and few visitors hang around for long after dusk.

WHAT TO DO

SPORTS

The long, white, sandy beaches and well-equipped marinas of the coast, combined with the mild climate, make watersports the obvious choice for an active holiday. Inland however, and in the delta of the Ebro River, there is a variety of other sports and activities to choose from.

Watersports

Several beaches, including Platja del Miracle and Platja Llarga (both in Tarragona), Salou, Calafell, Sitges, Cunit, Comaruga and Torredembarra offer sailing and windsurfing. Jet World in Amposta (tel: 977 703839; www.jet world2000.com) organises jet-ski trips on the Ebro River.

Kitesurfer in action at L'Hospitalet de l'Infant

Boats are for hire at many of the 22 marinas *(ports esportius)* dotted along the coast, for example Cambrils Charters (tel: 977 369642; www.cambrilscharter.com).

For canoeing in the water channels of the Ebro Delta contact Natura I Aventura at Sant Carles de la Pàpita (tel: 977 742987; www.naturayaventura.com) or for the white waters inland in the Sierra de Montsant, Canoa Kayak Siurana at Cornudella de Montsant (tel: 606 414223).

Getting a suntan

Seeing the Ebro by boat

Biking

The flattest place for cycling is around the Ebro Delta. Firms hiring out bikes here include Comercial Torne in Deltebre (tel: 977 480017).

If you're after more challenging terrain, Montroig del Camp, inland from Cambrils, is one of nine designated 'mountain bike centres' in Catalonia offering 100km (60 miles) of sign-posted routes. The information point is open summer Mon–Sat 9am–2pm and 4.30–7pm, Sun 9am–2pm, winter Sat–Sun only (tel: 977 810978; www.mont-roig.oasi.org).

Fishing

Spain has a regional and local, rather than national, licensing system and the kind of *licencia de pesca* you'll need depends on where exactly you want to fish. The best place to ask about this is in a tackle shop on the spot – they will probably also help you fill out the application form. For more information contact the Federacion Catalana de la Pesca, Calle Béjar 59, Barcelona, tel: 93 289 3300, www.fcpeic.com.

Hiking and Climbing

Tarragona province has some magnificent countryside to explore on foot. Even without leaving the coast you can walk a stretch of the GR 92 long-distance footpath which runs from the French border to Ulldecona, passing by Salou and Cambrils, L'Ametlla de Mar and across the Ebro estuary. The best walking country is, however, inland in the mountains around Prades and in the Ports de Beseit near Tortosa which rise to over 1,400m (4,600ft). Both areas are magnificent examples of wild Mediterranean landscape with forests of holm oak and pine, and cliffs and crags inhabited by mountain goats and overflown by vultures and golden eagles. Wherever you go, take water with you and a hat to protect you from the sun.

This is also one of the best rock-climbing regions in all Spain, the great rock walls of El Falco, Arboli and Siurana, and those of the Sierra de Montsant being veritable meccas of the sport.

Birdwatching in the Ebro Delta

The Ebro Delta (*see pages 60–4*) gets large numbers of tourists and the best times for serious birdwatching are weekdays out of the holiday season. The most sensitive parts of the reserve cannot be visited without permission but public access is permitted to other parts and if you are prepared to walk, cycle or drive for kilometres up sand or dirt tracks you can sometimes find satisfactory sites away from humanity. Before venturing anywhere ask for a map at either of the two information offices. The main one is in Deltebre village (tel: 977 489679; Mon–Fri 10am–2pm and 3–6pm, Sat 10am–1pm and 3–6pm, Sun and public holidays 10am–1pm; www. deltebre.org). The information office for the southern part of the reserve is the Casa de Fusta (tel: 977 261022; Mon–Sat 10am–2pm and 3–7pm, Sun and public holidays 10am–2pm), which is next to l'Encanyissada lagoon.

Golf

Good clubs in the region include: Reial Club de Golf El Prat, in Barcelona; the Costa Daurada, set amid rolling countryside northeast of Tarragona (closed to non-members at weekends); Reus Aiguësverd, between Reus and Cambrils; and Bonmont Terres Noves, northwest of Cambrils. For more information contact the Real Federación Española de Golf, tel: 91 555 2682, www.golfspainfederacion.com.

Bar in Barcelona

ENTERTAINMENT

Nightlife

You can find most types of nightlife on the Costa Dorada. It's at its most sophisticated in Barcelona and Sitges, and at its most basic in the mass-market resorts of Salou and Callella. As yet Tarragona has little to offer the tourist.

Sitges by night is bohemian and gay in every sense (though by no means exclusively so, *see pages 36–40*). At weekends it fills up with trendy, young Barcelonans. Clubs and late-night bars are always popular, and perhaps the only drawback here is that there are surprisingly few quiet nightspots. The town's most notable club is Atlántida, principally because it's an open-air venue (www.clubatlantida.com).

Salou, meanwhile, resounds with Euro-pop and karaoke. If you are staying on the Costa del Maresme, you are within easy reach of similar entertainment as at the Gran Palace Lloret (at Lloret de Mar on the Costa Brava). You certainly won't be alone at either of these places, as each holds around 1,500 people.

Barcelona is one of the world's greatest cities when it comes to nightlife, with entire guidebooks devoted solely to its plethora of 'designer bars', clubs and concert halls. If you don't want to venture out in Barcelona on your own, join an

Gambling

The only casino south of Barcelona is the Gran Casino de Barcelona, which is actually located at San Pere de Ribes, just west of Sitges. Grand it certainly is from the outside, with cypresses, fountains and gates leading to a 19th-century Catalan-Renaissance mansion, not unlike an imposing French château in style. The marble foyer is impressive, but the gaming room, slot machines and decor seem somewhat at odds with the opulence of a previous era. The casino games you can play here are roulette, la boule (a roulette-style game), baccara/chemin de fer, punto-banco and blackjack. Even if you're not gambling, it is fascinating to watch both clients and croupiers at work.

If you plan on going, you will need either your passport, identity card or driver's licence. A tie isn't necessary, but you should dress smartly. The casino also stages regular international cabaret and occasional outdoor classical music, dance and opera performances.

If you are staying on the Costa del Maresme, you will be in easy reach of its sister casino, the more modern Casino de Lloret, which offers the same games, albeit in less salubrious surroundings.

The facade of the Liceu
in Barcelona

organised coach tour. These depart frequently from Costa Dorada resorts during the summer months, and after a tour of the floodlit sights of the city, usually end up at a flamenco show.

Concerts, Opera, Ballet

If it's the performing arts you want, then a trip to Barcelona is usually necessary. The city's 140-year old Gran Teatre del Liceu is one of Europe's finest theatres. It can be visited for tours (La Rambla, 51–59; tel: 93 485 9900; charge). The opera house has been completely renovated and extended after a disastrous fire in 1994.

Another Barcelona concert hall worth an admission fee in its own right is the Palau de la Música de Catalana, which is arguably the city's finest example of *Modernisme* architecture.

Aside from these two major venues, there are many more for which tickets are easier to obtain. Ask at a tourist office.

As far from the big city lights as possible is the monastery of Santes Creus (36km/22 miles from Tarragona, *see page 70*). Performances of classical and church music are occasionally held here in the atmospheric dormitory.

Cinema

Film buffs will know that each October, Sitges hosts an International Festival of Fantasy and Horror Films. If you want to see a film with its original soundtrack, look for the letters 'v.o.' *(version original)*.

SHOPPING

Although you can find almost anything you want in Barcelona, it can be very time consuming to do so, especially when there are so many other sights to see. You can always combine shopping and sightseeing in the Poble Espanyol, where artisans will make a candlestick to order, or blow glass while you wait. Barcelona has long been an expensive town for shopping, and Sitges is not far behind, while Salou is mostly cheap and cheerful. For individuality and a more reasonable price range, the side streets of Tarragona, and the off-the-beaten-track villages and small towns are probably your best bet.

Best Buys

With the general evening out of prices between Spain and the rest of Europe, genuine good bargains are now few and far

Many shops in Barcelona bear Modernist trademarks

between. Aim to come home with something stylish and different, rather than something which is simply cheaper.

Leatherware. A cottage industry along the coast produces a multitude of leather goods. Handbags, purses and clothing are the main items. Price and quality vary widely, so look closely and shop around before buying. The same applies to shoes.

Jewellery. Either simple, modern designs, or traditional with lots of silver or gold filigree.

Embroidery, lace, basketwork and woven goods. There are all kinds of home-spun goods in this category; you'll generally find hand-crafted items in villages.

Local wines and spirits. Take home a still wine from the Penedés region or a good-quality cava to remind you of Sant Sadurní d'Anoia; a bottle of the unique Aromes liqueur from Montserrat; or a Moscatel dessert wine.

Catalan ceramics. These may be either primitive or very sophisticated. *Azulejos*, decorative tiles of Moorish origin, are good (if heavy) souvenirs.

Antiques. Try Barcelona, Sitges or Tarragona. None is cheap, but Tarragona is likely to be the least expensive. Go to the antiques market held by the cathedral steps on a Sunday.

Castellers in Spain

The most spectacular of all Catalonia's many folklore celebrations is surely the art of the castellers. These are the men and boys who climb barefoot onto one another's shoulders to form human towers which reach up to nine storeys high. The most pampered participant is the young boy who scampers to the very top of the tower and takes the crowd's cheers. The unsung heroes, however, are those at the very bottom of the pile who hold the pyramid up.

Castellers appearances are fairly common, but try to catch them while you can. The team from Valls are acclaimed as being the kings of their art.

FOLKLORE AND FESTIVALS

Catalonia celebrates its festivals just as vigorously as the rest of Spain. There are so many of them that it's likely you'll encounter at least one in the vicinity during your holiday. Each and every festival is different, but there are also certain practices and rituals that are common to most.

Sardana

The best-known Catalan folklore expression is the dance known as the *sardana*. To the outsider this seems a sedate, perhaps even dull affair; but to a Catalan patriot it implies an uncommon degree of participation and a literal bonding between people of all ages.

Castellers reach dizzy heights with their human towers

A group joins together in a circle, hold their hands high, and to a musical accompaniment, alternate between slow, thoughtful steps and medium-tempo bouncy kicking. It's not really a spectator event, so once you know roughly what is going on, break into the circle (but not between the man and the lady to his right) and follow the dancers' example.

Music for the *sardana* (also called *sardana*) is played by a *cobla*, a wind band with double bass consisting of 12 instruments played by 11 musicians. Four of the instruments (tenora, tible, flabiol and tamborí) are typical Catalan instruments; the others (trumpet, trombone, fiscorn and double bass) are more conventional. In Spanish and French Catalonia about hundred thirty coblas are active, most of which are amateur orchestras.

Each *sardana* lasts for around 10 minutes. *Sardanas* take place at festivals, parties, family gatherings, or simply because it's the weekend.

Ball dels Bastons

A more specialist fiesta dance is the *ball dels bastons* ('dance of the sticks'). Men and boys wearing a kind of Morris-dancer costume beat sturdy, knuckle-bruising sticks together in a hybrid of dancing, fencing and jousting.

Gegantes at the Festes de la Verge de la Mercè, Barcelona

Gegantes and Capgrosses

A thoroughly Catalan and colourful *fiesta* characteristic is the presence of *gegantes* (giants) and *capgrosses* (big heads). The former are towering papier-mâché figures – kings and queens or lords and ladies – measuring up to 4.5m (15ft) high, which are controlled by skilled crews hidden beneath. As they march the streets, they may stop for a 'chat' with spectators leaning out of first-floor windows, before suddenly whirling full circle – much to the amusement (and no doubt consternation) of the crowds beneath them. The *capgrosses* are cartoon-like figures with large, papier-mâché heads, who play the part of jesters complementing the stately *gegantes*.

Devils and Dragons

A Spanish *fiesta* is nothing without fireworks, and in Catalonia this is the cue for the entrance of *diables* (devils) and *el drac* (the dragon). The devils are men and boys dressed in sackcloth costumes with horns and tails. Above their heads they hold special, wooden frames, on which they rotate flaming fireworks as they march through the crowd. If this sounds a little alarming, then look out for the dragon: pausing only to grab a mouthful of fresh firecrackers and explosive devices, the dragon crew charge through the narrow streets, spewing fire and sparks in all directions and scattering the crowd with excited yelps.

It's easy to see in advance what route the dragon will take, since shopkeepers board their windows in order to prevent firework damage. It's both deafening and great fun, but do protect your eyes and keep small children at a safe distance.

Flamenco

One of Spain's best-known entertainments is *flamenco* – throbbing guitars, stamping heels and intense songs that well up from the soul. Many of the songs resemble the wailing chants of Arab music, which may indicate Moorish origins.

Flamenco is very much an Andalusian art form and is therefore quite foreign to Catalonia, but numerous *tablaos* (floorshows) are staged in tourist spots and hotels.

There are two main types of flamenco song: the first, bouncy and cheerful, is known as *cante chico*; the other, dark and soulful, is the *cante jondo*, performed in the slow, piercing, melodramatic style of the great flamenco artists.

CHILDREN

Long, sunny days and soft, sandy beaches mean that the Costa Dorada is a favourite family destination. Off-beach options for older children are limited, but many hotels have

Kids' Stuff in Barcelona

There's plenty for children in Barcelona. The **Barcelona Zoo** is acclaimed as one of Europe's finest. The Aquarium, at the harbour, is another good animal attraction. There is also a **3-D Imax** movie theatre in the port. Your children may enjoy the **Poble Espanyol**, where there is always something going on in the streets and squares, or the hands-on **science museum** (at 47–51 Carrer Teodor Roviralta). If the fair seems like more fun, then visit either the **Parc d'Atraccions Montjuïc**, or the **Parc d'Atraccions Tibidabo**. Both have first-class rides and occupy hilltop locations with marvellous views (you'll need a clear day to appreciate Tibidabo). The **cable-car** up to Montjuïc is a wonderful ride in its own right and definitely should not be missed. Tibidabo, which is even higher, is reached by taking the city's last remaining tramcar, the *tramvia blau*, up the hill, where you change to the funicular railway. In terms of funfair attractions, Tibidabo may have the edge.

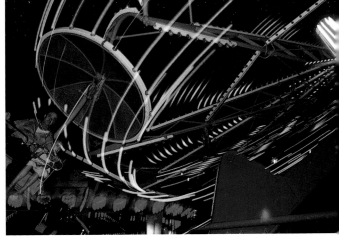

Parc d'Atraccions Tibidabo

special features for the young, ranging from child-minding to supervised poolside games.

On the whole, nightlife for the kids on the Costa Dorada isn't very organised, but there are few, if any, restrictions on children coming out with you to bars and restaurants. Large hotels may also organise children's evening activities.

When the appeal of splashing in seawater and building sandcastles starts to wear thin, try some of the following:

Port Aventura

One of the biggest theme parks in Europe, Port Aventura is organised into the five 'lands' of China, Mexico, Polynesia, the Far West and the Mediterranean, and makes a great family day out. The park has a variety of rides, shows and other attractions. The most spectacular rides are the Dragon Khan roller coaster with eight upside-down loops to endure, and the Hurakan Condor, which allows visitors

Playing with dolphins will
delight youngsters

to experience a free fall from
the equivalent of 42 storeys
high. There are also a number
of more sedate attractions for
younger children, including
puppet shows and an old-
fashioned carousel.

Also part of Port Aventu-
ra is the Caribe Aquatic Park
(*see below*) and two hotels.

Make a Splash

Waterparks are a popular
activity off the beach. You'll
find **Acquapark** (the biggest) at La Pineda (next to Salou).
Others include: **Aquatic Paradis**, just outside Sitges;
Marineland, at Palafolls on the Costa del Maresme; **Aqua-
leon** in Albinyana, near El Vendrell, which is also a zoo;
and the **Caribe Aquatic Park**, part of Port Aventura. At Acquapark, while the kids hurl themselves down the
'kamikaze' or ride the 'super toboggan', you can sunbathe
in the landscaped gardens. Additional park attractions include mini-golf and ten-pin bowling. Marineland also features dolphins, performing parrots and seals, and many
more animals.

Go-Karting

Go-kart tracks are common along the coast. Karting Salou
on the Salou–Reus road features karts which are styled to
look like Formula One racing cars. There are high-speed
karts for adults, a children's kart circuit for the over-4s, and
no danger of selecting the wrong gear, since the karts don't
have any. Being low to the ground, they cannot tip over,
while at the same time they give a great sensation of speed.

Festivals

Each town and village celebrates the national holidays, but the main festival, the *festa major*, is held on the local saint's day, which varies between areas. After the *sardanas*, *gegantes*, *diables*, *el drac* and so on, a street dance is usually held. The larger towns pulsate well into the early hours with Latin rhythms, while a no-expense-spared firework display illuminates the sky.

February/March Sitges: *Carnaval* – combines the best of Rio- and Catalan-style celebrations. Sitges: International Vintage Car Rally.
March/April Montserrat, Poblet: *Semana Santa* (Holy Week, week preceding Easter) – processions and religious celebrations in all towns.
April Barcelona: *Diada de Sant Jordi* (St George's Day, also birthday of Miguel de Cervantes) – book fairs, and the Day of Lovers. Whole region: feast day of Virgin of Montserrat (27 April).
May Callella: *Festes de Primavera* (Spring Festival) – folk-dancing, vintage cars, bands.
May/June Sitges: *Festes del Corpus Christi* – streets are strewn with flowers; music, dancing, fireworks.
June Callella: *Aplec de Sardanas* – folk-dance festival. Valls: Dia de Sant Joan (24 June) – folklore and *castellers*.
July Arenys de Mar: *festa major* – celebrations at sea and ashore.
August Valls: *Festes del Firagost* (Assumption) – harvest celebrations, folklore, religious procession; Vilafranca del Penedés: *festa major* – religious procession and *castellers*.
September *La Diada* (11 September) – Catalonia's national day is celebrated by everyone throughout the region. Barcelona: *Festes de la Verge de la Mercè* (Our Lady of Mercy; around 24 September) – celebrations combine traditional festivities with an international festival of theatre, song, dance and music of all types. Tarragona: *Festa major* (de *Santa Tecla*) – religious and folklore spectacles, including *castellers*.
September/October Sitges, Tarragona: *Festes de la Verema* (grape-harvest festival) – tastings, dancing and competitions.

EATING OUT

The Catalans take their food seriously, and you will rarely be disappointed by the choice, flavour or hearty portions served up at restaurants along the Costa Dorada. If you don't want a full restaurant meal, there's still plenty of authentic local choice — from *tapas* in a bar, to chicken and *cava* in a fast-food style *pollo al'ast* (barbecued chicken) outlet.

Restaurants

Throughout Spain, restaurants are graded by a 'fork' system. One fork is the lowest grade, five forks is the highest. These ratings, however, are awarded according to the facilities and degree of luxury offered, and not the quality of the food. (See page 136 for a list of recommended restaurants.)

All restaurants should offer a *menú del día* (day's special). This is normally three courses, including wine, at a very reasonable set price. The prices on the menu usually include taxes and a service charge, but it is customary to leave a tip if the service was good.

Two notes of caution: *tapas* prices are not always indicated, and can be surprisingly expensive, so always ask before you order. Also ask how much the bill will be when ordering fish or seafood, priced by the kilo. The price depends on the uncooked weight and can be very expensive.

Meal times are generally later in Spain than in the rest of Europe. Peak hours are generally from 2 to 3.30pm for lunch and 9.30 to 11pm for dinner. If you get hungry during the day, you can always have *tapas* in any bar.

For a comprehensive guide to the vagaries of the menu in Spanish restaurants, there is the Berlitz *Spanish-English/English-Spanish Pocket Dictionary* or the Berlitz *European Menu Reader*.

Café de Reus in Canet de Mar

Bars and Cafés

From sunrise to the middle of the night, from the first coffee to the last brandy, the Spanish café is a very special institution. In practice there is little difference between what is a bar and what is a café, aside from the bias of the bar towards alcoholic drink.

Bars and cafés are the meeting places for both locals and tourists, either to swap the day's news in pidgin-English, Spanish or German, or shout animatedly at the football on television. The price of a cup of coffee buys you a ring-side seat for as long as you want.

Wines and spirits are served at all hours all over Spain, so don't be surprised if you see someone knocking back a large measure of colourless fire-water first thing in the morning. You may also be surprised to see children frequenting bars with impunity. The Spanish consider this quite natural, even late at night.

Bars and cafés, like restaurants, usually include a service charge, but additional small tips are the custom if you have spent any time in the establishment. Prices are 10–15 percent lower if you stand or sit at the bar rather than occupy a table.

> ### Portion control
>
> *Una tapa* is the smallest amount; *una ración* is a small plateful. Try to keep your enthusiasm in check. It is quite easy to spend more on *tapas* than on a good restaurant meal.

Tapas

A *tapa* is a small portion of food to accompany your drink. The word *tapa* means 'lid', and comes from the old custom of giving a free bite of food with a drink – the food being served on a saucer on top of the glass, like a lid. Nowadays it is fairly rare to see *tapas* given away – perhaps the odd olive or peanut.

Bonafide *tapas* bars, and indeed many simple bars, have a whole counter display of hot and cold *tapas*, which makes choosing very easy. You can simply point to the one you like the look of. Some of the most common *tapas* you'll find are meatballs (*albóndigas*), olives (*aceitunas*), local cheese (*queso*), Russian salad (*ensaladilla rusa*), tortilla de patatas (wedges of potato omelette), octopus salad (*pulpo*), prawns in garlic (*gambas al ajillo*), mushrooms (*chamínones*), *jamón serrano* (mountain-cured ham) and *chorizo* (paprika-spiked salami-style sausage).

Tapas are always accompanied by a small basket of fresh bread or Catalan-style *pa amb tomaca* (bread with tomato). The bread is rubbed with garlic, then smeared with tomato, grilled, and then drizzled with olive oil.

Breakfast

For Spaniards, breakfast is the least significant meal of the day and will probably just consist of *tostada* (toast) or *pa amb tomaca*, and coffee. If you have a sweet tooth, look out for places selling *churros (xurros)*. These are batter fritters, extruded into long strips, deep-fried and sugared. If you want to be taken for a native, dunk them in your coffee or hot chocolate (more of a thick sauce than drinking chocolate).

Most hotels offer breakfast buffets with an international mélange of cereals, fresh and dried fruits, cheese, cold meats, plus bacon and eggs. Several cafés cater for the tourist by offering a full breakfast *(desayuno completo)* of orange juice, bacon, eggs and all the other trimmings.

Catalan Cuisine

There have been several influences on the cuisine of Catalonia and the Costa Dorada. The rich, sauce-based recipes of the South of France filtered down via the Costa Brava, while the abundant rice crops of the Ebro Delta, and Valencia's

Attentive service in Cambrils

famous *paellas* wafted up from the south. The sea harvest is a rich source of inspiration, while recipes from the Pyrenees suggest warm, filling peasant food.

There are also national favourites such as *gazpacho* (pronounced gath-PACH-o), a delicious chilled soup, made with chopped tomatoes, cucumbers and garlic, and served with crouton. It's a great refresher on a hot summer day.

The classic dish *paella* (pronounced pie-ALE-ya), is named after the black iron pan in which the saffron rice base is cooked in stock. Various combinations of squid, prawns, shrimps, rabbit, chicken, mussels, onion, peppers, peas and so on are added, according to what type of *paella* is on the menu. It's always cooked to order (usually for a minimum of two people) and is a feast for the eyes as well as the taste-buds. In addition to the above, look out for the following Catalan dishes:

Bacalao or Bacallà. Salt-cod, surprisingly not a local, but fished from far-off northern waters. It was salted originally to preserve it, and it's vital that the cod is soaked first to remove the salty taste. Today refrigeration has replaced the salt's preservation role, but salting is still employed in order to impart a distinctive flavour. *Bacallà* is served in numerous ways – one is *Bacallà amb samfaina*, in a sauce resembling ratatouille.

Fishy Business

The province of Tarragona has long been famous for the quality of its fish, and just as wine has a nominated area quality control, so too does fish.

In this case the denomination is *Peix Blau*, literally meaning 'blue fish', although a better translation would be 'blue label'. Look for the crates as they come off the boats, anywhere in the region, and you will see this rating.

Fish at the market

Escalivada. An olive-oil dressed cold salad of grilled or baked vegetables, including peppers and aubergines.

Escudella. A hearty meat and vegetable broth with beans, pasta, *chorizo*, chicken or veal. It's not common in tourist haunts, but off the beaten track and out of season you may come across it.

Esqueixada (pronounced es-kay-SHA-da). A stimulating salad of salt-cod, red pepper and tomatoes.

Fideuà. A plainer cousin of seafood *paella*, substituting noodles for rice and without many of *paella*'s more colourful ingredients.

Pollo al'ast. Barbecued chicken hardly qualifies as an authentic Catalan meal, but do look out for these flaming spit-roasted displays, often outside fast-food style establishments. A quarter of a chicken accompanied by a glass of *cava* (more likely to be a plastic cup) is one of the best value meals you can get in the resorts of the Costa Dorada.

Romesco. A sauce that is the pride of Tarragona. It's made of oil, ground almonds, hazelnuts, chilli, tomatoes, garlic and breadcrumbs, and is perfect for fried fish and shellfish.

Suquet de Peix. A rich seafood stew with onions, tomatoes, potatoes and brandy.

Xató (pronounced sha-TO). A salad speciality of Sitges, with anchovies, tuna or cod, and a spicy sauce of oil, vinegar, red pepper, anchovies, garlic and ground almonds, served with olives and endives.

Zarzuela. Another rich fish and seafood feast in a tomato and wine sauce.

Dessert

When it comes to dessert, the Catalans seem to lose their inventiveness. *Crema catalana*, made of eggs, sugar and milk, and flavoured with cinnamon and lemon, is a creamy cousin of the ubiquitous Spanish dessert, *flan*, with a hard, glassy caramelised crust. Aside from these, however, the choice is usually limited to ice cream *(helado)*. If you do get the chance, sample *mel i mató*, a simple (uncooked) mix of honey and fresh cream cheese. It's sold at the market stalls at Montserrat in small tubs, and occasionally finds its way onto restaurant menus.

Alcoholic Drinks

Both provinces of the Costa Dorada – Barcelona and Tarragona – produce good **wine**. The Penedés region *(see page 71)* is acclaimed for its excellent still wines, while the region around Sant Sadurni d'Anoía produces more sparkling wine by the *méthode champenoise* than anywhere in the world, including the Champagne region of France itself.

Torres is the most famous label of the Penedés area. This is largely a white-wine region but two of the best-known

Torres labels are on red wines – *Sangre de Toro* ('bull's blood') and the famous, award-winning *Gran Coronas Mas La Plana* (Black Label).

The large **cava** houses are Freixenet and Cordoníu *(see page 73)*, but there are many producers of excellent sparkling wine in the region. Cava is not only much cheaper than Champagne, it is also generally less acidic, and therefore appeals to a wider audience. Look for *brut* or *brut natur* on the label if you like it dry.

To the north of Tarragona, the Priorato region is well known for its full-bodied red wines; look for the *Scala Dei* label.

Torres red wine is one of the best produced in Penedès

Tarragona and Sitges are known for sweet **dessert wine**. The latter make fortified dessert wines in the same *solera* system used to produce sherry. Try also a Moscatel to accompany your dessert. A good one will have a delicious sultana and honey flavour.

When you visit Montserrat, be sure to have a taste of the excellent **liqueur**, *Aromes de Montserrat*, which is made by the monks.

Sangría is probably the most popular tourist drink in Spain. It is a mixture of red wine, orange and lemon juice, brandy and lemonade, with lots of sliced fruit and ice added.

La Boqueria in Barcelona has several good places to eat

Beware, though, this perfect hot-weather concoction can pack quite a punch.

Beer *(cerveza)* on the Costa Dorada can be any of a number of quality lager brands – *Damm* is recommended. If you want a small beer, ask for *una caña*. *Una cerveza grande* may be about the same size as a British pint.

Tea, Coffee and Soft Drinks

The Spanish usually drink **coffee** *(café)* as opposed to **tea** *(té)*. This can be either *solo* (small and black); *con leche* (large with milk, often capuccino-style); or *cortado* (a small cup with a little milk). Spanish coffee is nearly always strong and tasty. If it is too strong, ask for *un americano*, a weak coffee, or *descafeinado* if you want it caffeine-free.

Mineral water *(agua mineral)* is either sparkling *(con gas)* or still *(sin gas)*. Ice-cream parlours sell *granizado* –

slushy, iced fruit juice in several flavours, as well as *zumo de naranjas* – freshly pressed orange juice. The latter is surprisingly expensive given the fact that it is one of Spain's main crops.

You may also come across *horchaterías*, which specialise in the cool, very Spanish refresher, *horchata de chufa*. It's a milky drink made from a fruity, wrinkled little nut with a sweet, almondy taste.

To Help You Order…

Could we have a table?	**¿Nos puede dar una mesa?**
Do you have a set menu?	**¿Tiene un menú del día?**
I'd like a/an/some…	**Quisiera…**

beer	**una cerveza**	potatoes	**patatas**
bread	**pan**	salad	**una ensalada**
coffee	**un café**	sandwich	**un bocadillo**
dessert	**un postre**	soup	**sopa**
fish	**pescado**	sugar	**azúcar**
ice cream	**un helado**	tea	**un té**
menu	**la carta**	(iced) water	**agua (fresca)**
mineral	**agua**	wine	**vino**
water	**mineral**		

… and Read the Menu

aceitunas	olives	**arroz**	rice
ajo	garlic	**asado**	roast
albari-		**atún**	tuna
coques	apricots	**bacalao**	salt cod
albóndigas	meatballs	**besugo**	sea bream
almejas	baby clams	**bistec**	beef steak
anchoas	anchovies	**caballa**	mackerel
anguila	eel	**calamares**	squid

callos	tripe	judías	beans
cangrejo	crab	langosta	lobster/ crayfish
caracoles	snails		
cebollas	onions	lenguado	sole
cerdo	pork	limón	lemon
champi- ñones	mushrooms	lomo	loin
		manzana	apple
chorizo	a spicy pork sausage	mariscos	shellfish
		mejillones	mussels
chuleta	chops	melocotón	peach
cordero	lamb	merluza	hake
dorada	seabass	naranja	orange
ensalada	salad	ostras	oysters
entre- meses	hors- d'oeuvre	pastel	cake
		pescado	fish
estofado	stew	pescadilla	whiting
filete	fillet	pez espada	swordfish
flan	crème caramel	pimiento	capsicum peppers
fram- buesas	raspberries	piña	pineapple
		plátano	banana
fresas	strawberries	pollo	chicken
frito	fried	postre	dessert
galletas	biscuits (cookies)	pulpo	octopus
		queso	cheese
gambas	shrimp/ prawns	salchichón	salami-type sausage
granadas	pomegranates	salmonete	red mullet
guisantes	peas	salsa	sauce
helado	ice cream	sandía	watermelon
hígado	liver		
higos	figs		
huevo	eggs		
jamón	ham		

HANDY TRAVEL TIPS

An A–Z Summary of Practical Information

A

ACCOMMODATION (see also CAMPING, YOUTH HOSTELS, and the list of RECOMMENDED HOTELS on page 129)

Most accommodation in the Costa Dorada is of a medium international standard, with a predominance of two- and three-star hotels. Hotels are the norm, but apartments and aparthotels may be found in the more popular coastal resorts. Hotels are government-inspected and graded 1–5 stars depending upon facilities. Hostels *(hostales)* are modest hotels with few facilities and are denoted by the sign H. Pensions (*pensiones*, boarding houses denoted by the letter P) are the most basic form of accommodation. Both *pensiones* and *hostales* are graded 1–3 stars. The letter R, suffixed to a hotel or hostel sign, indicates *residencia*, where there is no restaurant. *Paradores* are state-run establishments, sometimes set in historic buildings, whose aim is to provide the chance to experience 'the real Spain' and to reflect the indigenous style. The only *parador* on the Costa Dorada is at Tortosa.

Most accommodation in resorts such as Salou is in reasonably priced 2–3-star hotels and apartments. Sitges, on the other hand, caters for a more chic crowd, including weekend Barcelonans, and is therefore quite expensive. The Costa del Maresme resorts are also popular with Barcelonans. Barcelona itself is very expensive;

I'd like a double/single room	**Quisiera una habitación doble/sencilla**
with/without bath/shower double bed	**con/sin baño/ducha cama de matrimonio**
What's the rate per night?	**¿Cuál es el precio por noche?**
Is breakfast included in the room rate?	**¿Está incluído el desayuno?**
Where's an inexpensive hotel?	**¿Dónde hay un hotel económico?**

Tarragona has a fair choice, but there is a lack of good medium-priced accommodation. As a general rule, book ahead whenever possible.

When checking in to a hotel, you will be asked to surrender your passport for a short period. In general, prices are quoted per room (as opposed to per person). Value added tax (IVA) of 7 percent is added to the bill (13 percent at 5-star hotels).

AIRPORTS (aeropuertos)

Charter flights for resorts near Tarragona use the airport at Reus, 19km (12 miles) north of Tarragona; a few scheduled flights arrive here also. Barcelona's modern international airport is at El Prat de Llobregat (www.aena.es), 15km (9 miles) from the city centre. The national train service, **RENFE** (tel: 902 240202), runs trains from just outside the airport. They leave every half hour, stopping at Estació de Sants and Plaça Catalunya, taking about 20 minutes. The fare is around €5. The **Aerobús** departs every 15 minutes from all three terminals for Plaça de Catalunya, stopping at numerous points en route. The fare is €4.50 (ticket valid for a week). **Taxis** charge about €20–25 to the centre of the city.

B

BUDGETING FOR YOUR TRIP

Barcelona is, on the whole, more reasonable than other major European cities, such as London, Paris or Rome. Tarragona is cheaper, and the various other destinations along the Costa Dorada vary according to their popularity.

Transport. For Europeans, Barcelona is a short, direct flight away. As well as regularly scheduled flights there is a good choice of discounts and charter flights, especially those booked on the Internet with budget airlines. For those travelling from beyond Europe, the flight will be a considerably greater proportion of your overall budget.

Accommodation. Hotels in Barcelona, along with Madrid, are the most expensive in Spain, but many at the three- and four-star level are comparatively good value. Out of Barcelona, it really depends which destination you choose *(see page 106).* See approximate prices in the 'Recommended Hotels' section, starting on page 129. It is always wise to book ahead.

Meals. Restaurant prices, particularly in Barcelona, are not cheap, though with a favourable exchange rates, even top-rated restaurants may be surprisingly affordable compared to many European capitals. The *menú del día,* a fixed-price midday (and sometimes evening) meal, is an excellent bargain available in most towns and resorts. Spanish wines are an excellent deal.

Local transport. Public transport within and between the cities, whether by bus or train, is reasonably priced. Taxis are an affordable way to get around the cities.

C

CAMPING *(camping)*

The Costa Dorada has many officially approved campsites. For information, contact the Federació Catalana de Campings (tel: 93 285 1980; www.campingsonline.com/costadaurada).

Camping grounds are divided into four categories (luxury, 1st-, 2nd- and 3rd-class) and rates and facilities vary accordingly. All sites have drinking water, toilets and showers, electricity, medical facilities and safes for valuables, and are attended night and day.

CAR HIRE (RENTAL) *(coches de alquiler* – see also DRIVING)

Car-hire companies in Barcelona and along the Costa Dorada offer a wide range of cars at varying prices. If you want to book in advance you can contact virtually any major car-hire company.

Major international companies – Avis, Hertz, Budget, National – and Spanish companies have offices in Barcelona airport and in the city centre. A value-added tax (IVA) of 15 percent is added to the total charge, but will have been included if you have paid before arrival (normally the way to obtain the lowest rates). Fully comprehensive insurance is required and should be included in the price; confirm that this is the case. Most companies require you to pay by credit card, or use your card as a deposit/guarantee.

You must be over 21 and have had a licence for at least six months. A national driver's licence will suffice for EU nationals; others need an international licence.

I'd like to rent a car (tomorrow)	**Quisiera alquilar un coche (para mañana)**
for one day/a week	**por un día/una semana**
Please include full insurance.	**Haga el favor de incluir el seguro a todo riesgo.**
unleaded petrol	**gasolina sin plomo**
Fill it up.	**Lleno, por favor.**

CLIMATE AND CLOTHING

Climate. Sunbathers can enjoy the beaches of the Costa Dorada for about five months of the year. The mild climate throughout the rest of the year still provides a pleasant break from chilly Northern Europe and is ideal for sports.

		J	F	M	A	M	J	J	A	S	O	N	D
max	°F	55	57	60	65	71	78	82	82	77	69	62	56
	°C	13	14	16	18	21	25	28	28	25	21	16	13
min	°F	43	45	48	52	57	65	69	69	66	58	51	46
	°C	6	7	9	11	14	18	21	21	19	15	11	8

Clothing. In addition to summer- and beach-wear, don't forget sweaters or wraps for evenings. For the excursion to Montserrat *(see page 66)* you may need warmer clothing and sturdy shoes.

Casual wear is the norm, though if you intend to frequent expensive hotels or restaurants, the opera house, theatre or the casino, then a jacket and tie (though not obligatory) may be advisable.

Topless bathing is quite common, but cover up off the beach. Shorts and mini-skirts should not be worn when visiting religious sites.

COMPLAINTS

By law, all hotels and restaurants must have official complaint forms *(Hojas de Reclamaciones)* and are obliged to produce them on demand. The original of this document should be sent to the Ministry of Tourism, one copy remains with the establishment involved, and one copy is given to the person who is making the complaint.

Try to resolve the problem before going through this procedure, as in practice it is difficult to pursue any claims once you have left the area. The very action of asking for the *hoja*, however, may resolve the problem in itself, as tourism authorities often view malpractice seriously, and can revoke or suspend licences.

You should also inform the local tourist office, or in serious cases the local police, of any complaints, and seek their assistance.

CONSULATES *(consulados)* AND EMBASSIES *(embajadas)*

The consulates listed below are all in Barcelona, which is also the location of consulates representing almost all other Western European countries. Citizens of Commonwealth countries may also call on the UK consulate. All embassies are located in Madrid.

Canada: Elisenda Pinós, 40; tel: 93 204 2700
Ireland: 10th Floor, Gran Via Carles III, 94; tel: 93 491 5021
South Africa: Parc Empresarial Mas Blau II Alta Ribagorra, El Prat de Llobregat, tel: 93 506 9100

UK: Avinguda Diagonal, 477; tel: 93 366 6200
US: Passeig Reina Elisenda de Montcada, 23; tel: 93 802 2227

Where is the British/ American Consulate? It's very urgent.	**¿Dónde ésta el consulado británico/americano? Es muy urgente.**

CRIME AND SAFETY (see also LOST PROPERTY)

Crimes involving violence against tourists are rare. The most common crime is theft from hire cars. If you park overnight in the street in one of the big towns or resorts, there is every chance that your car will be broken into.

Thieves also operate at tourist locations where cars are left unattended. Never leave anything of value in your car at any time. Hotels recommend that you use the safe deposit box in your room – for which there is usually a charge – for all valuables, including your passport. Burglaries at holiday apartments do occur, so keep doors and windows locked when you are absent and while you are asleep.

Beware of pickpockets, particularly in crowded places, such as markets or bus stations, or on the Barcelona Metro. If you are visiting Barcelona, be particularly vigilant on the lower section of Las Ramblas and beware of street sellers. You must report all thefts to the local police for your own insurance purposes.

I want to report a theft.	**Quiero denunciar un robo**

CUSTOMS AND ENTRY REQUIREMENTS

Most visitors, including citizens of all EU countries, the US, Canada, Ireland, Australia and New Zealand, require only a valid passport – no visa, no health certificate – to enter Spain. Visitors from South Africa must have a visa.

If you expect to remain for longer than 90 days (US citizens 180 days), a Spanish Consulate or tourist office can advise you.

Although there is no restriction on what you may bring in with you as a tourist, you are likely to find the same items cheaper in Spain.

By law, visitors must declare sums over €6,000 that they are bringing into Spain.

D

DRIVING

Arrival. If you want to bring your own car to Spain, you will need the car registration papers, a nationality plate or sticker, a red warning triangle, a Green Card extension to your regular insurance policy, and a bail bond which can be arranged through your insurance company. Your own driver's licence is valid in Spain, but you may want to obtain an International Driver's Permit for extra assurance.

Driving conditions. Drive on the right, overtake on the left and yield right of way to all vehicles coming from your right. Horns are officially banned inside cities.

Main roads are very good and even country roads are well surfaced. The A7 *autopista* (motorway) winds inland from Barcelona before heading south west, parallel to the coast, all the way to the Costa del Azahar. This is an excellent, fast road, but beware of hefty tolls and the fact that some junctions do not allow both entrance and exit. If you do intend using the *autopista*, it's worth looking for a map that gives details on junction restrictions or you can be stuck on the motorway for several kilometres before you can exit. Beware, too, of driving near a big city on a Sunday evening. Massive traffic jams build up, both on and off the motorway, as Barcelonan weekenders head back from the beach.

Driving and parking is tolerable in Tarragona, but is certainly not recommended in the centre of Barcelona, although a through-road system has greatly improved the journey across the city. It is advisable to study maps carefully before setting off.

Parking. Metered parking is quite common in both large and small towns. Your car will be towed away if you park illegally in Barcelona. It is an offence to park the car facing against the traffic.

Traffic police. Armed civil guards *(Guardia Civil)* patrol the roads on motorcycles. In towns the municipal police handle traffic control. If you are fined for a traffic offence, you will have to pay on the spot.

Rules and regulations. Always carry your driving licence and/ or International Driving Permit with you. As the police can demand to see your passport at any time, it is also a good idea to carry a photocopy of its important pages (if not the actual passport itself) with you.

Spanish law requires that your car should carry a set of spare head-lamp and rear-lamp bulbs, and a reflective yellow jacket to wear in case of a roadside emergency. Motorcyclists and pillion riders must wear crash helmets and motorcycle lights must always be switched on. Seat belts are compulsory when driving outside built-up city areas. Children under the age of ten must travel in the rear.

Breakdowns. Spanish garages (look for the sign 'Taller') are efficient and spare parts are readily available for most makes of car. If you are an affiliated member of the RAC, you may call on the services of the *Reial Automòbil Club de Catalunya*, who are at: Gran Via de les Corts Catalanes 187, 08004 Barcelona, tel: 93 495 5000; and Rambla Nova 114, Tarragona, tel: 977 211962.

Road signs. Aside from the standard pictographs you may encounter the following (these are in Castilian Spanish, but you may see them in Catalan):

Aparcamiento	Parking
Autopista (de peaje/peatge)	(Toll) motorway
Ceda el paso	Give way (Yield)
Despacio	Slow
Desviación	Diversion (Detour)
Estacionamiento prohibido	No parking
Obras	Roadworks
Peatones	Pedestrians
Peligro	Danger
Salida	Exit (from motorway)

Driving licence	**Carné de conducir**
Car registration papers	**Permiso de circulación**
Green Card	**Carta verde**
Can I park here?	**¿Se puede aparcar aquí?**
Are we on the right road for…?	**¿Es esta la carretera hacia…?**
Fill the tank please, top grade.	**Llénelo, por favor, con super.**
Check the oil/tyres/battery.	**Por favor, controle el aceite/ los neumáticos/la batería.**
I've broken down.	**Mi coche se ha estropeado.**
There's been an accident.	**Ha habido un accidente.**

E

ELECTRICITY (corriente eléctrica)

220-volt current is the norm, though if you are in an old building in the countryside, you may find 125-volt current. If in doubt, ask.

EMERGENCIES (urgencias)

National/municipal police	**091**
Guardia Civil	**062**
Fire brigade	**080**
National emergency number	**112**

Fire	**Fuego**
Help!	**¡Socorro!**
Stop!	**¡Deténgase!**
Stop thief!	**¡Al ladrón!**

ETIQUETTE

The people of Catalonia are generally hard-working and hospitable and enjoy meeting visitors from other countries. A little under-standing of their society and etiquette will go a long way to getting what you want from them and making friends. Athough many peo-ple who live here are from other parts of Spain, most people you are likely to meet will be native Catalans. As such, they may resent being called Castilian Spanish – they may even prefer to speak Eng-lish than Spanish – and they will be impressed if you show knowl-edge of their distinct history and culture. A large part of the population has Catalan as its first language and if you can manage a few words of this it will be taken as a sign of your respect.

Even if you can't master the local language, be aware that po-liteness and common courtesies matter greatly. Always begin any conversation, even if you are only asking for directions, with *bon dia* ('good morning') or *bona tarda* ('good afternoon'). Likewise, when entering a shop, office or public place always say a general hello to those present. Sign off with *adéu* ('goodbye').

G

GETTING TO THE COSTA DORADA

By air *(see page 107)*. A charter flight into Reus can still be the cheapest way to get to the Costa Dorada, but with the arrival of low-cost airlines scheduled flights have become extremely competitive. They usually operate more frequently and depart and arrive at more sociable hours – important if you intend to use public transport. The two big operators are easyJet (www.easyjet.com) which flies into Barcelona and Ryanair (www.ryanair.com) which flies into Reus. Surprisingly good deals can also be had from regular scheduled airlines such as Iberia (www.iberia.com), the Spanish national carrier, and British Airways (www.british-airways.com). The flight from London to Reus takes about 2 hours.

Some transatlantic flights go direct to Barcelona but there will be more choice if you go via Madrid and change on to a domestic flight.

By road. The main access road from France to the Costa Dorada is at the eastern side of the Pyrenées. You can join the A7 *autopista* at the frontier post of La Jonquera, 150km (93 miles) north of Barcelona. An alternative route from Toulouse, over the Pyrenées, enters Spain at Puigcerdà and follows the N152 route for 169km (105 miles) to Barcelona. The scenic route is the coast road from the Port Bou border post along the Costa Brava.

By rail. The 'Trenhotel' links Paris with Barcelona in 12 hours. From there, change at Sants Station for the coastal line to Tarragona and beyond. For most other connections, you'll have to change trains at Port Bou on the border of France and Spain.

Inter-Rail cards are valid in Spain. For further information contact Rail Europe, 1 Regent Street, London SW1 (tel: 08448 484 064; www.raileurope.com). The Spanish National Railways, RENFE (*Red Nacional de los Ferrocarriles Españoles*; tel: 902 240202; www.renfe.es) also offers unlimited rail travel passes. RENFE's official representative in the UK is the Spanish Rail Service (tel: 020 7725 7063; www.spanish-rail.co.uk).

GUIDES AND TOURS

Tour operators run coaches on various day trips along the Costa Dorada. Depending on where you are staying, you will be able to choose from the following: Poblet and Santes Creus, Tarragona, Barcelona (by day and by night), Montserrat (combined with a visit to a *cava* producer), Andorra and Peñiscola (Costa del Azahar). Costa del Maresme operators also run several trips to the Costa Brava. Commentaries are given in all major languages, though it never harms to specify the language you require at the time of booking.

Tours can be booked through your hotel reception and most travel agents. If you would like a personal guide to a particular place, the tourist office should be able to direct you to local guides and tell you their rates.

H

HEALTH AND MEDICAL CARE

EU residents should obtain the EHIC (European Health Insurance Card), which entitles them to free medical treatment within the EU. It is unwise to travel without health insurance as treatment can be expensive.

Many tourists from northern climes often suffer painful sunburn through overdoing it on the first day or two. Falling asleep on the beach is a common cause. Take the sun in short doses for at least the first few days, and go easy on the alcohol as well. Spirits are poured in liver-crippling measures and the beer also packs a punch. Drink plenty of bottled water *(agua mineral)* to avoid dehydration.

A list of doctors who speak your language is available at local tourist offices. There are hospitals in all the principal towns and a first-aid station *(casa de socorro)* in smaller places.

Pharmacists *(farmacias)* are recognisable by a green cross sign and are open during normal shopping hours. After hours, at least one per town – the *farmacia de guardia* – remains open all night. Its address is posted in the window of the other *farmacias*. *Parafarmacias* look like chemists and sell over-the-counter medicines, but they don't sell prescription drugs.

Where's the nearest (all-night) pharmacy?	**¿Dónde está la farmacia (de guardia) más cercana?**
I need a doctor/dentist.	**Necesito un médico/dentista.**
I've a pain here.	**Me duele aquí.**
sunburn	**quemadura del sol**
sunstroke	**insolación**
a fever	**fiebre**
an upset stomach	**molestias de estómago**
insect bite	**una picadura de insecto**

L

LANGUAGE (see also MAPS AND STREET NAMES)

Both Catalan and Castilian Spanish are official languages in Catalonia. Catalan is a Romance language, with its roots in the French Langue d'Oc, which originated in the Provence area of France.

Regional policy and the personal preference of most Catalans is towards Catalan, but don't worry – the people you meet will also speak Castilian Spanish and often speak English too. Street signs are in Catalan; museum captions and menus are usually in both languages. In tourist areas English is often spoken, or at least understood, but using some courtesy phrases in Catalan will always go down well.

English	Catalan	Castilian
Good morning/Good day	**Bon dia**	**Buenos días**
Good afternoon/Good evening	**Bona tarda**	**Buenas tardes**
Goodnight	**Bona nit**	**Buenas noches**
Please	**Si us plau**	**Por favor**
Thank you	**Gràcies**	**Gracias**
You're welcome	**De res**	**De nada**
Goodbye	**Adéu**	**Adiós**

The Berlitz phrasebook *Spanish for Travellers* covers most situations you are likely to encounter during your travels in Spain. Here are a few useful words that may come in handy:

where/when/how	**dónde/cuándo/cómo**
how long/how far	**cuánto tiempo/a qué distancia**
yesterday/today/tomorrow	**ayer/hoy/mañana**
day/week/month/year	**día/semana/mes/año**
left/right	**izquierda/derecha**
up/down	**arriba/abajo**
good/bad	**bueno/malo**
big/small	**grande/pequeño**
cheap/expensive	**barato/caro**
hot/cold	**caliente/frío**
old/new	**viejo/nuevo**

LOST PROPERTY

Retrace your steps. If you still cannot find the missing item, report the loss to the Municipal Police or the Guardia Civil *(see page 122)*. They will issue you with a form of which you will need a copy if you wish to make an insurance claim once you are home.

I've lost my wallet/ handbag/passport.	**He perdido mi cartera/ bolso/pasaporte.**

MAPS AND STREET NAMES

One manifestation of the upheavals that post-Franco Catalonia has been undergoing is in the name of streets, many of which are being re-baptised, causing some confusion. Place and street names in

Catalonia are mostly met with today in their Catalan version. Here are a few Catalan street signs:

English	Catalan	Castilian
Avenue	**Avinguda**	**Avenida**
Street	**Carrer**	**Calle**
Church	**Església**	**Iglesia**
Palace	**Palau**	**Palacio**
Boulevard	**Passeig**	**Paseo**
Square	**Plaça**	**Plaza**

a street plan of...	**un plano de la ciudad de...**
a road map of...	**mapa de carreteras de...**

MEDIA

Newspapers and Magazines *(periódicos; revistas)*. Major British and Continental newspapers are on sale the same day as publication.

Radio and Television *(radio; televisión)*. Many hotels have satellite TV offering a variety of foreign channels. There are seven Spanish channels, most dedicated largely to sport, foreign films and game shows. Travellers with short-wave radios will be able to pick up the BBC World Service and the Voice of America.

Have you any English-language newspapers?	**¿Tienen periódicos en inglés?**

MONEY

Currency. The monetary unit of Spain is the euro (€); with one hundred cents making 1 euro. Coins: cents 1, 2, 5, 10, 20 and 50, and euros 1 and 2. Banknotes: euros 5, 10, 20, 50, 100, 200 and 500.

Banking hours are usually from 9am to 2pm, Monday to Friday. Banks in the popular resorts open longer hours and on Saturday at the height of the season.

Outside banking hours, many travel agencies display a *cambio* sign and will change foreign currency. Most hotels will also change money, albeit at a slightly less favourable rate than at the bank. Automatic Teller Machines *(cajeros automáticos)* are everywhere, and from them you can draw funds in euros against your bank account with a credit/debit card.

Traveller's cheques always get a better rate than cash. Take your passport with you when changing money or traveller's cheques.

Credit cards and **traveller's cheques** are accepted in most hotels, restaurants and big shops.

Where's the nearest bank?	**¿Dónde está el banco más cercano?**
I want to change some pounds.	**Quiero cambiar libras.**
Do you accept traveller's cheques?	**¡Acepta usted cheques de viaje?**
Can I pay with this credit card?	**¿Puedo pagar con esta tarjeta de crédito?**

OPENING HOURS

Opening and closing hours vary, but generally work around the lunchtime break; usual hours are from 9.30am–1.30pm or 2pm and 4.30pm–5pm or 8 pm.

Banks. 9am to 2pm Monday to Friday.

Bars and restaurants. Most restaurants open 1.30–4pm and 9–11pm, but in the resorts many bars open from noon or earlier until the small hours. Less formal restaurants open all day.

Museums. Times are variable, but most open between 10am and 1 to 2pm, and re-open from 3 or 4pm to 6 or 7pm. However, some go straight through from 10am to 5.30pm. Most close all day Monday.

Post offices. Provincial post offices open from 8 or 9am to noon or 1pm, and 4 or 5pm to 6 or 7pm Monday to Friday. Most open mornings only on Saturday. Tarragona's main office opens 8am to 9pm.

Shops. 9am to 1pm and 4 or 5pm to 7 or 8pm, Monday to Saturday. Some department stores and hypermarkets stay open at lunchtime.

P

PHOTOGRAPHY

All popular brands and types of camera batteries, digital camera cards and general accessories are sold on the Costa Dorada. Wherever possible, ask people for their permission before you take their picture. It is forbidden to take photographs of any military bases, military or naval port areas, police, government or military personnel.

POLICE *(policía)*

There are three police forces in Spain. The military police are called the *Guardia Civil* (Civil Guard). They patrol motorways and wear an olive-green uniform. Each town also has its own *Policía Municipal* (municipal police) who wear a distinct uniform depending on the

Where is the nearest police station?   **¿Dónde está la comisaría más cercana?**

town and season, but are mostly found in blue and grey. The third force, the *Cuerpo Nacional de Policía*, a national anti-crime unit, can be recognised by their light brown uniforms. Catalonia has its own police force called *Mossos d'Escuadra*. All police officers are armed. If you need police assistance you can call on any of these forces.

POST OFFICES

These are for mail and telegrams, not telephone calls. Stamps *(sellos)* are sold at any tobacconists *(estanco*, marked *tabacos)* and by most shops which sell postcards. Post boxes are painted yellow; the slot marked *estrangers* is for overseas mail.

Poste restante. If you don't know in advance where you will be staying, you can still have mail forwarded to you addressed *poste restante (apartado de correos)*, at whichever town is most convenient, i.e.: Mr John Smith, Apartado de Correos, Tarragona, Spain.

   When collecting you must take your passport to the post office as identification.

Where is the (nearest) post office?	**¿Dónde está la oficina de correos (más cercana)?**
Have you received any mail for…?	**¿Ha recibido correo para…?**
A stamp for this letter/postcard please.	**Por favor, un sello para esta carta/tarjeta.**
express (special delivery)	**urgente**
airmail	**via aérea**
registered	**certificado**

PUBLIC HOLIDAYS *(fiestas)*

January 1	*Año Nuevo*	New Year's Day
January 6	*Epifanía*	Epiphany

May 1	*Día del Trabajo*	Labour Day
June 24	*Día de Sant Joan*	St John's Day
July 25	*Santiago Apóstol*	St James' Day
August 15	*Asunción*	Assumption
October 12	*Día de la Hispanidad*	Discovery of America Day (Columbus Day)
November 1	*Todos los Santos*	All Saints' Day
December 6	*Día de la Constitución Española*	Constitution Day
December 25	*Navidad*	Christmas Day
December 26	*San Esteban*	St Stephen's Day

Movable dates

Jueves Santo	*Maundy Thursday*
Viernes Santo	*Good Friday*
Lunes de Pascua	*Easter Monday*
Corpus Christi	*Corpus Christi*
Inmaculada Concepción	*Immaculate Conception*

In addition to these Spanish national holidays, many other purely local holidays are celebrated in various towns *(see page 93)*.

PUBLIC TRANSPORT

Bus services. Buses in the region are cheap, reasonably comfortable and reliable, but beware of drastically reduced timetables on Sunday. They generally only run into and out of the provincial centres, so links to smaller resorts, even if they are quite close to each other, may not be possible.

There are regular buses from Tarragona to Salou and Cambrils (15–20 minutes), Poblet (75 minutes), Montblanc (60 minutes) and Barcelona (90 minutes).

Train services. A good service, linking all the main resorts and towns, runs right down the Costa del Maresme, through Barcelona, and along the Costa Dorada to Valencia. The Barcelona station serving the coastal line is Santis. Contact Spanish National Railways, RENFE, for timetable and ticket information (tel: 902 240202, www.renfe.es).

Taxis. The letters SP *(servicio público)* on the front and rear bumpers of a car indicate that it is a taxi. It will probably also have a green light in the front windscreen or a green sign indicating *libre* (free) when it is available for rent. Taxis are unmetered in tourist areas. Fares to the most popular destinations are fixed and displayed on a board at the main taxi rank. These are reasonable by European standards. If in doubt, ask the driver before you set off.

When is the next bus/train for…?	**¿A qué hora sale el próximo autobús/tren para…?**
I want a ticket to…	**Quiero un billete para…**
What's the fare to…?	**¿Cuánto cuesta el billete a …?**
first/second class	**primera/segunda clase**
single (one way)	**ida**
return (round trip)	**ida y vuelta**
Where can I get a taxi?	**¿Dónde puedo coger un taxi?**

R

RELIGION

The national religion of Spain is Roman Catholicism, and Mass is said regularly in almost all churches. In the principal tourist centres, services are also held in foreign languages. Inquire at the tourist office.

T

TELEPHONES *(telefonos)*

The cheapest and easiest way to make any sort of call, from local to international, is in a *locutorio teléfonico* kiosk. You go to a numbered booth, dial the number yourself, and pay the person at the desk who has metered your call. Alternatively, you can dial internationally from any street-corner telephone booth *(cabina)*. Pick up the receiver and when you get the dial tone, dial 07; wait for a second dial tone, then dial the country code, local code (minus the first zero) and then the number you are calling. You will need a plentiful supply of coins or a phone card *(tarjeta telefónica)*, which you can buy from a tobacconist. Easy-to-understand instructions in all languages are available to help you. Most bars have coin-operated or meter telephones available for public use as well.

If you must call home from your hotel (by far the most expensive option), ask in advance how much a 3-minute call will cost.

The country code for Spain is **34**. All provincial codes begin with **9**. Numbers in Barcelona and Sitges begin with **93**, followed by a seven-digit number. Most other numbers in Tarragona and Costa Dorada begin with **977**, followed by a six-digit number. Even for local numbers you must include the provincial code.

For national directory inquiries dial **11888**; for the international operator dial **11886**.

TIME DIFFERENCES

Spanish time coincides with that of most of Western Europe – Greenwich Mean Time plus one hour. In late March, clocks are put forward an hour, and put back one hour in late October.

New York	London	Spain	Sydney	Auckland
6am	11am	**noon**	8pm	10pm

TIPPING

Service is normally included in bills; the following are just suggestions.

Hotel porter, per bag	50 cents
Maid, per week	€2
Waiter	10 percent
Taxi driver	10 percent

TOILETS

The most commonly used expression for toilets is *servicios* or *aseo*, though you may also hear or see *WC*, *water* and *retretes*. Public conveniences are rare, but all hotels, bars and restaurants have toilets.

TOURIST INFORMATION *(oficina de turismo)*

Spanish National Tourist Offices *(oficinas de información turística)* are maintained in many countries. See also www.spain.info.
Canada: 2 Bloor Steet West, Suite 3402, Toronto, Ontario M4W 3E2, tel: 416 961 3131
UK: PO Box 4009, London W1A 6NB, tel: 020 7486 8077; visits to the office must be booked in advance
US: 8383 Wilshire Boulevard, Suite 960, 90211 Beverly Hills, CA 90211, tel: 323 658 7195; 666 5th Avenue, 35th floor, New York, NY 10103, tel: 212 265 8822

Every town of any reasonable size on the Costa Dorada has its own tourist office. The offices at Tarragona are at Carrer Major, 39, www.tarragonaturisme.cat for the province, and at Carrer Fortuny, 4, www.catalunyaturisme.com for the whole of Catalonia.

TRAVELLERS WITH DISABILITIES

Provisions for disabled travellers on the Costa Dorada are not great, but since the 1992 Barcelona Paralympics awareness of their needs has at least been raised. There are wheelchair ramps at the airports, and many larger apartments and hotels make provision for guests with disabilities. Salou has by far the greatest number of hotels with wheelchair facilities. Another three in Cambrils also claim facilities. Youth hostels at Deltebre, El Masnou (Costa del Maresme) and Barcelona are also suitable for wheelchair users.

Further details of accessible accommodation are given in Holidays and Travel Abroad, published by RADAR, 12 City Forum, 250 City Road, London EC1 8AF, tel: 020 7250 3222, www.radar.org.uk.

In the US, contact the Society for the Advancement of Travel for the Handicapped, 347 Fifth Avenue, Suite 605, New York NY 10016, tel: 212 447 7284, www.sath.org.

Other sources of information are the Spanish National Tourist Office *(see page 127)* and the Federation ECOM, which is a group of private organisations for the disabled; Gran Via de las Corts Catalanes 562-2a, 08011, Barcelona, tel: 93 451 5550, www.ecom. es. They also publish an Access guide to Barcelona.

W

WEBSITES

Useful websites to help with the planning of your holiday include:
www.bcn.es Barcelona's excellent official site
www.gencat.cat Catalonia on the web
www.spain.info The official Spanish tourism website
www.tarragonaturisme.cat Tarragona tourism website

YOUTH HOSTELS *(albergue de juventud)*

There are youth hostels at the following locations: **Costa del Maresme:** Cabrera de Mar and El Masnou. **Barcelona:** 3 hostels. **Costa Dorada** (south of Barcelona): El Vendrell, Altafulla, Tarragona, Deltebre. **Inland:** L'Espluga del Francolí.

For more information, contact Red Española de Albergues Juveniles, Calle Castelló 24, 28001 Madrid, tel: 91 522 7007, www.reaj.com.

Recommended Hotels

Below is a selection of accommodation in different price ranges for popular resorts and towns on the Costa Dorada. Book hotels well in advance, particularly if visiting in high season or during a fiesta period. The star rating in parentheses after each entry refers to the official government grading system *(see Accommodation on page 106)*. As a basic guide to room prices, we have used the following symbols (for a double room with bath/shower during the high season). Do be aware, however, that out of high season, room rates usually fall sharply.

€€€€	over 150 euros
€€€	100–150 euros
€€	50–100 euros
€	below 50 euros

BARCELONA

Hotel Colón €€€€ (4 stars) *Avenida Catedral, 7, tel: 93 301 1404, fax: 93 317 2915, www.hotelcolon.com.* This charming building boasts an unbeatable location opposite the cathedral and was one of Miró's favourite haunts. Ask for one of the two front rooms overlooking the cathedral plaza, where *sardanas* are danced every Sunday. Parking. 145 rooms.

Hotel España €€€ (2 stars) *Sant Pau, 9–11, tel: 93 318 1758, fax: 93 317 1134, www.hotelespanya.com.* A jewel of *Modernisme*, decorated by Lluís Domènech i Montaner, the España is recommended if you're looking for atmosphere. Even if the hotel is full, come here for a meal in their splendid restaurant. Located next to the Gran Teatre del Liceu. 69 rooms.

Hotel Gótico €€€€ (4 stars) *Jaume I, 14, tel: 93 315 2211, fax: 93 268 9062, www.gargallohotels.com.* Attractive, and well placed in the Barri Gòtic. The rooms are sound-proofed and have airconditioning; some have terraces. Parking. 81 rooms.

Hotel Gran Vía €€€ (3 stars) *Gran Vía de les Corts Catalanes, 642, tel: 93 301 7692, fax: 93 318 9997, www.nnhotels.es.* This delightful, 19th-century palace is full of old-world charm. The public rooms are richly furnished and decorated throughout with antiques and Art Nouveau fittings. Wheelchair access. 53 rooms.

Hotel H10 Gravina €€€€ (3 stars) *Gravina, 12, tel: 93 301 6868, fax: 93 317 2838, http://hotel-gravina.com.* Conveniently situated near Plaça Catalunya, the Gravina's classical façade conceals a very modern interior. The rooms are on the small side but spotlessly clean. Wheelchair access, parking. 84 rooms.

Hotel Husa Oriente €€€€ (3 stars) *La Rambla, 45–47, tel: 93 302 2558, fax: 93 412 3819, www.hotelhusaoriente.com.* Barcelona's most venerable hotel still preserves its former glamour and style. The ballroom incorporates part of an old Franciscan monastery, and there are two classical-style banquet rooms. The rooms are large and comfortable. 142 rooms.

Hotel Suizo €€€€ (3 stars) *Plaça de l'Angel, 12, tel: 93 310 6108, fax: 93 315 0461, www.gargallo-hotels.com.* Just off Vía Laietana, on the edge of the Barri Gòtic, the Suizo enjoys a prime location. Its recently renovated rooms, each with its own balcony, are spacious, bright and cheerful. 50 rooms.

SITGES

Galeón Hotel €€€ (3 stars) *Sant Françesc, 46–48, tel: 93 894 0612, fax: 93 894 6335, http://hotelsitges.com.* Small, friendly and slightly old-fashioned hotel, nestling in the narrow back streets of the town centre. Private, enclosed garden with a palm-shaded swimming pool. 47 rooms. Open May–October.

Hesperia Calipolis Hotel €€€€ (4 stars) *Avda Sifia, 2–6, tel: 93 894 1500, fax: 93 894 0764, www.hotelcalipolis.com.* This elegant, modern 11-storey hotel overlooks the main beach and provides every comfort in its well-appointed, spacious rooms. Attractive open-air terraces lead out to the promenade. 170 rooms.

Hotel Antemare €€€€ (4 stars) *Verge de Montserrat, 50, tel: 93 894 7000, fax: 93 894 6301, www.antemare.com.* Six apartment-like buildings make up the elegant Hotel Antemare, established for over 60 years in the heart of the town's quiet residential district. Two swimming pools and extensive fitness facilities are available. Wheelchair access. 117 rooms.

Hotel Platjador €€€ (3 stars) *Passeig de la Ribera, 35–36, tel: 93 894 5054, fax: 93 811 0384, http://hotelsitges.com.* Recommended for its beach-side location, pool and the views from its fifth-floor bar and lounge. 59 rooms. Open April–October.

Hotel Romàntic €€€ (2 stars) *Sant Isidre, 33, tel: 93 894 8375, fax: 93 894 8167, www.hotelromantic.com.* Three 19th-century villas have been combined to form a gem of a hotel in the quiet back streets of Sitges. Modernist architecture blends with old Cuba in the public areas and the delightful garden and bar. Very popular with the gay community. 58 rooms.

Hotel San Sebastián Playa €€€–€€€€ (4 stars) *Port Alegre, 53, tel: 93 894 8676, fax: 93 894 0430, www.hotelsansebastian.* A small, attractive and very well-equipped hotel, overlooking the quieter beach in Sitges. It's tastefully decorated throughout with smart and simple rooms. There's also a small swimming pool, a terrace, and a good restaurant. 48 rooms, all with balconies.

Hotel La Santa María €€€ (3 stars) *Passeig de la Ribera, 52, tel: 93 894 0999, fax: 93 894 7871, www.lasantamaria.com.* On the seafront, in the busiest part of town, the Santa María offers renovated and attractive rooms, traditionally furnished lounges and an excellent restaurant. Helpful, friendly owners. 57 rooms. Closed 16 December–14 February.

Hotel Subur €€€ (3 stars) *Passeig de la Ribera, tel: 93 894 0066, fax: 93 894 6986, www.hotelsubur.com.* Next door to the Santa María, this is a comfortable hotel with airconditioned rooms and friendly, helpful staff. Ask for a room at the back to escape the road noise. Good restaurant. 95 rooms.

Hotel Subur Marítim €€€€ (4 stars) *Passeig Marítim, tel: 93 894 1550, fax: 93 894 0427, www.hotelsuburmaritim.com.* An attractive, small, modern hotel with a spacious garden and swimming pool. Located in the quiet residential part of Sitges, but on the seafront and close to the town centre. 45 rooms.

Hotel El Xalet €€ (2 stars) *Isla de Cuba, 35, tel: 93 811 0070, fax: 93 894 5579.* A gorgeous, late 19th-century Modernist building which contrasts High Gothic with Art Nouveau. Lovely swimming pool and garden, and a charming period dining room. Rooms have antique furniture and all mod cons, including airconditioning. 11 rooms.

Sitges Park Hotel €€€ (3 stars) *Calle Jesús, 16, tel: 93 894 0250, fax: 93 894 0839, http://sitgesparkhotel.com.* Behind the street entrance of this very central hotel is a fairy-tale Gothic tower which is part of the original building, plus a beautiful palm-shaded terrace and swimming pool. Rooms are fairly basic. 85 rooms. Open 20 March–2 November.

ALCANAR

Tancat de Codorniu €€€–€€€€ (no classification) *Ctra N-340, Km 1059, tel: 977 737194, fax: 977 737231, www.tancatdecodorniu. com.* This 14th-century country house, close to the beach, was the summer residence of King Alfonso XII. The bedrooms are spacious and decorated in a modern style, creating a relaxing atmosphere. At the front of the hotel there is a porch opening on to the garden, with fruit trees and a swimming pool. 10 rooms.

ALTAFULLA

Hotel Gran Claustre €€€€ (no classification) *Cup, 2, tel: 977 651557, fax: 977 600757, www.granclaustre.com.* In the heart of the historic quarter, this former convent built in 1732, next to the castle walls, has been refurbished respecting the original features and wrought ironwork. The roof terrace provides panoramic views of the Mediterranean and the local castles. 20 rooms.

Hostal Noria € (2 stars) *Plaza La Font, 53, tel/fax: 977 238717.* If you want to stay centrally on a tight budget, these are quite possibly the best of the cheap rooms in this popular backpacker's area. 24 rooms. No credit cards.

Hotel Astari €€ (3 stars) *Vía Augusta, 95, tel: 977 236900, fax: 977 236911.* A comfortable hotel which is well located to visit the Roman monuments. Pleasant swimming pool and terrace bar with sea views as well as outdoor dining. 80 rooms.

Hotel Lauria €€ (3 stars) *Rambla Nova, 20, tel: 977 236712, fax: 977 236700, www.hlauria.es.* This comfortable and modern hotel is in the city centre, close to the Roman amphitheatre, and only a few metres from the delightful Balcó del Mediterrani *(see page 55).* No restaurant. 72 rooms.

Hotel Nuria €€ (3 stars) *Vía Augusta, 217, tel: 977 235011, fax: 977 244136, www.hotelnuria.com.* Modern hotel with restaurant and bar. Handy for the Platja de l'Arabassada. Good value out of season. 57 rooms.

Hotel Urbis €€ (3 stars) *Plaza Corsini, 10, tel: 977 240116, fax: 977 243654, www.hotelurbiscentre.com.* A member of the Best Western Hotel chain, the centrally located Urbis provides a good international standard of comfort. Restaurant. 44 rooms.

Sant Jordi €€ *Vía Augusta, 185, Playa Sabinosa, tel: 977 207515, fax: 977 207632, www.hotelsantjordi.info.* Conveniently located on Sabinosa beach, just outside Tarragona city, this modern hotel with sea views is popular with families and business people. 39 rooms. Bedrooms have internet connection.

H10 Salou Princess Hotel €€€ (3 stars) *Avenida de Andorra, tel: 977 382201, fax: 977 383410, www.h10.es.* Located on the town's quieter stretch of beach, but still close to the centre and to Port Aventura theme park. Well-equipped rooms and attractive sun terraces as well as swimming pools draw a cosmopolitan crowd. Wheelchair access. 327 rooms.

Hotel Planas €€ (3 stars) *Plaza Bonet, 3, tel: 977 380108, fax: 977 380533.* The Planas is modern and comfortable (though with modest public areas), and despite being in the centre of town, retains a quiet atmosphere. Meals are served on the attractive tree-shaded terrace. 100 rooms. Open April–October.

CAMBRILS

Cambrils Princess Hotel €€€€ (4 stars) *Carretera de Salou a Cambrils, tel: 977 364283, fax: 977 365351.* This smart hotel is set in a relatively quiet location on the main road, 2km (1½ miles) from both Salou and Cambrils, and only a few metres from the beach. Attractive swimming pool, plus sun terraces, tennis court and crazy golf. Popular with tour operators. Wheelchair access. 400 rooms.

Hotel Hesperia Centurión €€–€€€ (4 stars) *Avenida Diputació, 70, tel: 977 361450, fax: 977 361500, www.hesperia-centurion.es.* Smart, modern beachside hotel, surrounded by pines, set half-way between Salou and Cambrils. Comfortable, attractive rooms. Swimming pool and sun terrace, good restaurant. 211 rooms.

Hotel Mónica €€€ (4 stars) *Galcerán Marquet, 3, tel: 977 791000, fax: 977 793678, http://hotelmonica.com.* A comfortable, small hotel in the quiet back streets, yet close to the centre. Bright rooms and lawned garden with palm trees and outdoor pool; wheelchair access. Squash court, crazy golf. 100 rooms. (Half-board minimum tariff in high season.) Closed mid-December–mid-January.

Hotel Princep €€ (3 stars) *Narcís Monturiol, 2, tel: 977 361127, fax: 977 363532, www.hotelprincep.com.* Comfortable family-run hotel in the centre of town. Terrace and solarium plus restaurant. 27 rooms.

Hotel-Restaurante Rovira €€–€€€ (3 stars) *Avenida Diputació, 6, tel: 977 360900, fax: 977 360944, http://hotelrovira.com.* The 1960s façade of this hotel conceals a modern interior with a smart restaurant. 60 modest rooms. Closed during January.

Hotel Tropicana €€ (2 stars) *Avenida Diputació 33, tel/fax: 977 360112.* Modest, quiet, comfortable small hotel set on the main road close to the centre of Cambrils and opposite the beach. Attractive lawn with swimming pool. 30 rooms. Open March–mid-October.

Maritim Princess €€–€€€ (3 stars) *Avenida Diputació, 172, tel: 977 385596, fax: 977 384980, www.princess-hotels.com.* Large beachside apartment blocks, 2km (1½ miles) from Cambrils, with swimming pools, large sun terraces, tennis courts, sauna and children's playground. Popular with tour operators. Wheelchair access. 472 rooms.

LA PINEDA

Golden Donaire Park €€€ (3 stars) *El Vaporet, s/n, tel: 977 371066, fax: 977 371150, www.goldenhotels.com.* A beach chain hotel, convenient for families, very close to the town centre and to Port Aventura theme park. Most of its rooms have excellent views of the La Pineda's seafront and of the sea. 410 rooms.

TORTOSA

Parador de Tortosa €€€ (4 stars) *Castell de la Suda, tel: 977 444450, fax: 977 444458, www.parador.es. (Bookings can be made via Keytel in the UK, tel: 020 7616 60300, www.keytel.co.uk).* A beautifully restored medieval castle in a majestic position overlooking the town, cathedral and Ebro Valley. Public areas are a bit gloomy, but the rooms are comfortable and in local rustic style. Swimming pool. 72 rooms, 3 suites.

Recommended Restaurants

We appreciated the food and service in the restaurants listed below. If you find other places that you think are worth recommending, we would be pleased to hear from you. To give you an idea of the price for a three-course meal per person, without wine, we have used the following symbols:

€€€€ over 40 euros
€€€ 30–40 euros
€€ 20–30 euros
€ below 20 euros

It's advisable to book in advance for dinner at all establishments during high season. Book also for lunch in Barcelona restaurants. (The recommended Barcelona restaurants below are all centrally located.)

BARCELONA

Agut €€–€€€ *Gignàs, 16, tel: 93 315 1709.* Quality Catalan cuisine in an intimate setting which harks back to the 1930s. Excellent *menu del día*. Very popular, with queues and staff hurrying you along.

Amaya €€€€ *Rambla Santa Mònica, 20-24, tel: 93 302 1037, www.restauranteamaya.com.* Some of the best Basque cooking in the city can be found at this friendly establishment. Particularly good on Sunday. Look out for *cocochas a la vasca* (Basque barbels) and *chipirones del norte* (baby squid).

Can Culleretes €€ *Quintana, 5, tel: 93 317 3022, www.culleretes. com.* This family-owned restaurant, founded in 1786, is an institution in Barcelona and the second oldest in Spain. It is located in the Barri Gòtic, near the Rambla and the port, and offers good-value Catalan cuisine.

Can Majo €€€€ *Almirall Aixada, 23, tel: 93 221 5455.* An intimate and very popular fish restaurant in a rather seedy part of La

Barceloneta. Try the *arroz a banda* or the excellent paella. Closed Sunday night, and Monday during festivals.

Los Caracoles €€€ *Escudellers, 14, tel: 93 302 3185*. Opened in 1835, this restaurant *típico* is a minor legend in the Barri Gòtic, and serves classic Catalan cuisine at a reasonable price. It's patronised by opera and theatre personalities, whose signed photographs decorate the walls.

El Gran Café €€€–€€€€ *Avinyó, 9, tel: 93 318 7986*. A delightful, 1920s-style restaurant on two floors, close to the Rambla, serving French and Catalan food. Pianist in the evenings. Closed all day Sunday and in August.

Els Pescadors €€€€ *Plaza Prim 1, tel: 93 225 2018, www.els pescadors.com*. Located on a pretty square at the heart of the former industrial and fishing district of Poblenou, which is being rapidly gentrified. It has two dining rooms: the original one, which has been renovated, and a new, more modern one. In summer you can eat outside on the terrace. As the name suggests, it specialises in fish dishes.

Les Set Portes €€€ *Passeig de Isabel II, 14, tel: 93 319 3033, www.7portes.com*. A venerable institution, now designated an architectural monument and little changed since it opened in 1836. A reasonably priced, extensive menu of Catalan food served to up to 1,000 diners in any of the restaurant's seven rooms, from 1pm to 1am daily.

SITGES

Cal Pinxo €€€€ *Passeig de la Ribera 5-6, tel: 93 894 8637, www. calpinxositges.com*. A charming restaurant/art gallery on the seafront which serves good quality Mediterranean cuisine including a delicious selection of salads. A good place to sample *arroz negro*, *fidegua* or *langostinos*.

El Greco €€–€€€ *Passeig de la Ribera, 70, tel: 93 894 2906*. Local and international dishes served in comfortable surroundings here, in one of the town's best restaurants. Try carpaccio of venison on the seafront terrace. Closed Monday and Tuesday in summer, and 10 days in November.

Mare Nostrum €€ *Passeig de la Ribera, 60, tel: 93 894 3393*. Long-established, elegant but informal seafront restaurant, with a pleasant terrace and an attractive nautically themed dining room. Regional dishes include shrimp romesco, hake with cava, chicken and crayfish. Closed Wednesday, and 15 December–31 January.

Maricel €€€€ *Passeig de la Ribera, 6, tel: 93 894 2054, http:// maricel.es*. Charming restaurant near the cathedral, specialising in meat and fish dishes. Friendly staff. Closed Tuesday evening, Wednesday lunchtime and 1–15 November.

La Masía €€€ *Passeig Vilanova, 164-166, tel: 93 894 1076*. Splendid, traditional farmhouse setting with garden terrace. Personalities from near and far come for the huge portions of excellent local food.

El Posit €€€ *Port Alegre, 53, tel: 93 811 3620*. With a privileged position on the beach, El Posit offers fish and seafood dishes of the best quality with fresh ingredients coming directly from the market in Vilanova. Try the rice soup with lobsters. It has a new branch in town on the Playa de San Sebastián.

La Santa María €€€€ *Passeig de la Ribera, 52, tel: 93 811 0999*. The most popular place in town – the front terrace of this seafront restaurant is always packed. Long menu, efficient service, huge portions, good at all times of the day. Try the paella or the *zarzuela*.

El Velero €€€€ *Passeig de la Ribera, 38, tel: 93 894 2051, www. restaurantevelero.com*. Fine dining in elegant semi-formal surroundings on the seafront. Excellent fish dishes; start with salmon, elvers and crab, and try the prawns in peach sauce. Closed 22 December–22 January, Sunday in winter, and all day Monday (except during summer festivals).

TARRAGONA

Barquet €€€ *Gasómetro, 16, tel: 977 240023.* For more than 30 years the Solé brothers have been offering traditional Tarragona recipes prepared with the finest and freshest fish from the port. With a fine assortment of white wines at good prices. Wheelchair access. Closed Sunday, festival days, and August.

Cal Martí €€€ *Sant Pere, 12, El Serrallo, tel: 977 212384.* Famous for its seafood and authentic fisherman's dishes. Closed Sunday night, all day Monday, and for part of September.

La Caleta €€€ *Rafael Casanova, 24 (Paseo Marítimo), tel: 977 234040.* An elegant and distinguished chalet surrounded by pine trees with a terrace and ocean view. Catalan cuisine beautifully presented. Also very good fish and seafood, and chocolate mousse for dessert. Wheelchair access. Pets allowed. Closed Sunday nights, Mondays and in January.

Les Coques €€€ *Sant Llorenç, 15, tel: 977 228300.* Set in the historic quarter, Les Coques' modest portions and traditional yet cheery decor make a cosy refuge for a quiet dinner. Catalan specialities, Mediterranean cuisine and courteous service. Closed Sunday, one week in February and three weeks from late July–mid-August.

Les Fonts de Can Sala €€€ *Carretera de Valls (N240), 62, Saut Pere i Jaut Pau, tel: 977 288575.* An attractive restaurant in a traditional Catalan *masía* (farmhouse) decorated in rustic Catalan fashion and with the added delight of a lovely tree-shaded terrace. They specialise in typical Catalan cooking and *cuina de mercat* ('market cuisine'), which makes use of fresh inland produce. Closed Tuesday.

Fortí de la Reina Anna Stuart €€€ *Platja del Miracle, tel: 977 244877.* This restaurant, located in an old fortress, renovated and dedicated to Queen Anne Stuart, has a wonderful vaulted dining room and serves creative Mediterranean cuisine and a range of wines. From the terraces there are magnificent views of the sea and the city. Closed Tuesday, Sunday evening, January and 1–7 July.

Merlot €€ *Cavallers, 6, tel: 977 220652.* Located in an old section of town, it occupies a modernised ancient farmhouse with exquisite style depicting a collection of coffeepots and paintings of contemporary Catalan artists. Vast wine cellar and fine selection of cigars. Closed Sunday and Monday lunchtime in summer; Sunday night and Monday the rest of the year; 1–15 February and last week of December.

Morros €€€ *Passatge Rafael Campalans, 42, Torredembarra, tel: 977 640061, www.morros.es.* Located on the beach at Torredembarra, 14km (9 miles) north of Tarragona, this family-run restaurant serves Mediterranean cuisine with fish and seafood predominating. Try the *marisco al cava* (seafood with cava), *milhojas de sardinas con escalibada* (sardine pie with roast vegetables) or *taten de pera con cristal de caramelo* (pear pie with crystallised caramel).

Palau del Baró €€–€€€ *Santa Anna, 3, tel: 977 241464, www. palaudelbaro.com.* This renovated 19th-century mansion in the heart of the historic Tarragona has preserved its original frescoes and has a beautiful terrace for dinner or an aperitif. It has good value set menus on weekdays. Closed Monday.

La Puda €€ *Moll de Pescadors, 25, El Serrallo, tel: 977 211070.* A no-frills fisherman's café, with a cheerful area of gingham tablecloths set aside for more formal dining and a terrace. Try the *paella marinera*, the *sardinas a la brasa* or the black rice. Closed for dinner Sunday October–March.

Sol Ric €€€ *Vía Augusta, 227, tel: 977 232032.* This excellent, outdoor garden restaurant has been serving what many critics regard as the best food in Tarragona since 1959. Fish and shellfish dominate the menu, with romesco specials. Closed Sunday night, all day Monday, and 22 December–22 January.

El Tiberi €–€€ *Marti d'Ardenyà, 5, tel: 977 235403, http://eltiberi. com.* A very good value restaurant with a fixed-price help-yourself buffet. It is decorated in the style of a Catalan patio and the waitresses wear regional clothes. A good place to sample several traditional Catalan dishes at once. Close Sunday night and all day Monday.

Les Voltes €€ *Trinquet Vell, 12, tel: 977 230651.* A vaulted restaurant located under Tarragona's Roman Circus, serving Mediterranean cuisine backed up by good selection of wines. Try *bacalao con muselina de ajos* (cod in garlic sauce) or *rap al all cremat* (monkfish cooked with garlic).

SALOU

La Goleta €€€€ *Calle Gavina, tel: 977 383565.* Elegant restaurant facing onto the beach. Relax on the terrace at lunchtime or dine romantically by night inside. Spanish and international cuisine; try the lobster salad with avocados and the mango sorbet. Closed Sunday night.

VALLS

Masía del Plá €€–€€€ *Carretera del Valls C-37, km 19,00, tel: 977 630511, http://masiadelpla.com.* This restaurant, inland from Tarragona, has a cosy atmosphere and offers Catalan cuisine combined with more exotic products. It specialises in a wide variety of meat, including, rabbit, goat, lamb, quail and ostrich, *a la brasa*, cooked over a wood fire. This is one of the best place to try delicious snails, in different combinations.

CAMBRILS

Can Bosch €€€–€€€€ *Rambla Jaume I, 19, tel: 977 360019, www.canbosch.com.* This highly-renowned, stylish restaurant close to the port, started as a place for local fishermen to meet but has moved up-market since then. The menu is strong on fish and seafood which are treated with great creativity. Closed Mondays and Sunday evening.

Casa Joan Gatell €€€€ *Passeig Miramar, 26, tel: 977 360057.* This superb, seafront restaurant, which has been awarded a Michelin rosette, has been an institution in Cambrils since 1914. Fish and seafood par excellence feature prominently on the menu; try the *entremeses Gatell*, the bouillabaisse, or the *arroz marinera*. Ask for a table by the window on the first floor. Closed Sunday night, all day Monday and 15 December–15 January.

Gami €€€ *San Pedro, 9, tel: 977 361049*. A modern decor with a marine motif. Seafood cuisine with international flavour. Wheelchair access. Pets allowed. Closed Tuesday evenings, Wednesdays and Friday lunchtime.

Marina €€ *Passeig Miramar, 42, tel: 977 360432*. Attractive family-run seafront restaurant with a lovely terrace looking onto the harbour. Fish and seafood predominate. Closed Wednesday afternoon and all day Thursday, and 23 December–7 March.

Mas Gallau €€€€ *Cassetera N-340, km 1, tel: 977 360588*. Superb setting in an atmospheric re-creation of a beamed and stuccoed traditional Catalan *masía* (farmhouse). Extensive Spanish regional menu, try *escudella* followed by rabbit, or pig's trotters with escargots à la Catalane.

Rincón de Diego €€€€ *Carrer Drassanes, 7 – bajo, tel: 977 361307, www.rincondediego.com*. An elegant restaurant near the marina, specializing in innovative dishes based on Catalan cuisine. It offers a good selection of wines and cavas. Closed Monday, Sunday evening and 22 December–25 January.

L'ALBIOL

Mas Gibert €€–€€€ *Ctra. de l'Albiol, km 10,2; tel: 977 845153, http://masgibert.net*. This rustic-style restaurant is the perfect place to try *calçotades*, a typical Catalan dish, made with young white, home-grown onions. They are served on clay tiles, accompanied by a *porrón* of wine, and don't be surprised if you are offered a bib in order not to get your clothes dirty. It has a terrace with magnificent country views and a children's playground. Open Tuesday to Sunday for lunch only and Friday and Saturday evening.

INDEX

pocket guide

Costa Dorada

Third Edition 2009

Written by Paul Murphy
Updated and edited by Nick Inman
Series Editor: Tony Halliday

Photography credits
Conor Caffrey 69; Anabel Elston 101; Glyn
Genin 94; Paul Murphy 1, 62, 87; Mark Read 30,
34, 35; Neil Schlecht 17, 29, 32; Gregory Wrona
6, 8, 9, 10, 11, 12, 15, 18, 20, 22, 23, 24, 25, 26, 27,
33, 36, 37, 38, 41, 43, 44–5, 47, 49, 50, 52, 53, 54,
56, 57, 59, 61, 63, 66–7, 70, 71, 72, 73, 74, 75, 76,
77, 78, 79, 80, 82, 84, 85, 88, 91, 92, 95, 97, 102

Cover picture: 4Corners Images

Printed in Singapore by Insight Print
Services (Pte) Ltd, 38 Joo Koon Road,
Singapore 628990. Tel: (65) 6865-1600.
Fax: (65) 6861-6438

Berlitz Trademark Reg. U.S. Patent Office
and other countries. Marca Registrada

Every effort has been made to provide
accurate information in this publication,
but changes are inevitable. The publisher
cannot be responsible for any resulting
loss, inconvenience or injury.

Contact us

At Berlitz we strive to keep our guides as
accurate and up to date as possible, but if you
find anything that has changed, or if you have
any suggestions on ways to improve this guide,
then we would be delighted to hear from you.

Berlitz Publishing, PO Box 7910,
London SE1 1WE, England.
fax: (44) 20 7403 0290
email: berlitz@apaguide.co.uk
www.berlitzpublishing.com